QUASI-POLICING

Cavendish
Publishing
Limited

London • Sydney • Portland, Oregon

QUASI-POLICING

Leonard Jason-Lloyd
Senior Lecturer in Law, Coventry University,
Visiting Lecturer in Law, Scarman Centre,
University of Leicester and
Midlands Centre for Criminology
and Criminal Justice,
Loughborough University

Cavendish
Publishing
Limited

London • Sydney • Portland, Oregon

First published in Great Britain 2003 by
Cavendish Publishing Limited, The Glass House,
Wharton Street, London WC1X 9PX, United Kingdom
Telephone: + 44 (0)20 7278 8000   Facsimile: + 44 (0)20 7278 8080
Email: info@cavendishpublishing.com
Website: www.cavendishpublishing.com

Published in the United States by Cavendish Publishing
c/o International Specialized Book Services,
5824 NE Hassalo Street, Portland,
Oregon 97213-3644, USA

Published in Australia by Cavendish Publishing (Australia) Pty Ltd
45 Beach Street, Coogee, NSW 2034, Australia
Telephone: + 61 (2)9664 0909   Facsimile: +61 (2)9664 5420

© Jason-Lloyd, L   2003

British Library Cataloguing in Publication Data
Jason-Lloyd, Leonard
Quasi-Policing
1 Police – Great Britain
2 Criminal justice, administration of – Great Britain
I Title
345.4'1052

Library of Congress Cataloguing in Publication Data
Data available

ISBN 1-85941-836-8

1 3 5 7 9 10 8 6 4 2

Printed and bound in Great Britain MPG Books Ltd, Bodmin, Cornwall

ACKNOWLEDGMENTS

I wish to thank the staff at Cavendish Publishing for their help and support in the production of this book, especially Jeremy Stein and Jon Lloyd.

Very importantly, I wish to acknowledge the invaluable support of my wife, Usha.

I have endeavoured to state the law as at 31 March 2003.

Leonard Jason-Lloyd
April 2003

Author's note

On completion of the proof-reading of this book, it is apparent that this area of study is both vast and fast-moving; therefore, it is likely that a further edition may soon follow this first attempt to focus on the important issues raised by the subject-matter. In this respect, I hope I have succeeded, at least in part.

I am sure there may be a number of points that will invoke discussion and differences of opinion, especially in view of the wide and potentially volatile nature of this subject. Constructive observations will therefore be welcome from readers of this book and may be submitted via the publishers or direct to me at the following email address: lenjl@waitrose.com

CONTENTS

TABLE OF STATUTES

TABLE OF OTHER LEGISLATION

INTRODUCTION

This book is intended to enhance awareness of a rising trend that constitutes an important issue in modern times. Its principal focus is on the increasing use of civilians who have been given special powers under statute for the performance of specific public protection duties. Despite its significance, this evolving trend seems to have gone largely unnoticed, especially within a legal context.[1] Although significant research on the relationship between private security and public policing has been undertaken in recent years,[2] there is a lack of information on the specific subject covered in this book.

The term 'quasi-policing', as featured in the title, has been used to convey the fact that many hereto police and prison service functions are being devolved from these State bodies to specially empowered civilians. Therefore, this book focuses on the powers and duties of these civilians, who are performing certain functions more commonly associated with police and prison officers. These individuals are to be distinguished from the uniformed operatives engaged in *general* security duties, such as those who patrol or guard factory and building sites, office blocks, supermarkets and other commercial centres, as well as uniformed security guards employed on cash-in-transit duties, who operate from armoured vehicles.

General security operatives are primarily employed to protect the assets of the clients who utilise their services, and are therefore limited to ordinary citizens' powers in the course of their duties. These include the relevant powers to make arrests, in respect of arrestable offences, under s 24 and Sched 1A of the Police and Criminal Evidence Act 1984,[3] the common law power to prevent or deal with a breach of the peace, and s 3(1) of the Criminal Law Act 1967. Such powers come under the general heading of citizens' arrests and will be discussed in detail below. However, certain provisions under the Police Reform Act 2002 are beginning to change the overall balance between the powers of civilians and the police. This will be discussed at length in the second Part of this book.

Most of the operatives discussed here are part of the private security industry. Many of them are supplied by security companies that are among the market leaders in this field. In recent years, this industry has increased massively in size and scope, and the Private Security Industry Act 2001 was passed mainly in response to this continuing expansion. It was also enacted due to increasing concerns regarding a minority of rogue elements within the industry. These have inflicted disproportionate damage to the image and overall standing of the legitimate aspects of this activity. In view of the increasing size and responsibilities of the private security industry, the 2001 Act will be crucial in enhancing public confidence in the providers of private security services. This is particularly important in view of the specialised role of private security operatives who are specifically employed to perform public protection duties.

---

1   See Jason-Lloyd, L, 'Criminal justice legislation and the private security sector' (Parts I and II) in (1996) Criminal Lawyer, March/April, pp 5–7 and May/June, pp 4–8; and Jason-Lloyd, L, 'The devolution of public protection to the private security sector' (2001) 74(1) Police Journal, pp 68–71.

2   For a criminological perspective on this subject, see George, B and Button, M, *Private Security*, 2000, Leicester: Perpetuity; and Button, M, *Private Policing*, 2002, Devonshire: Willan.

3   This may also apply to the 'any person' arrest powers as illustrated in Appendix 3 (see below, p 109).

The Private Security Industry Act 2001, once fully in force, is intended to regulate the private security industry through a new body, named the Security Industry Authority (launched on 2 April 2003). Its principal duties will include the maintenance of a licensing and inspection regime, as well as other work related to improving general standards within the industry. The roles due to be regulated include manned guarding, already mentioned above, as well as key holders, security consultants, private investigators, door supervisors and even wheelclampers.[4] Currently, the Lord Chancellor's Department is endeavouring to include bailiffs within the ambit of regulation under the 2001 Act. A fuller account of the Private Security Industry Act 2001 will be made in the third part of this book.

The first Part of the book will portray the powers and duties attributable to civilians who are specially empowered to perform specific public protection duties. These special duties include security in magistrates' courts, airports, privately-managed prisons, the prisoner escort service, secure training centres and their escort arrangements, immigration removal centres and their escort arrangements, and security in and around the Channel Tunnel. There will also be coverage of civilian enforcement officers, created under the Access to Justice Act 1999 in order to execute routine arrest warrants instead of the police. Very importantly, discussion of all the above operatives will include a number of contentious legal points concerning their powers.

The second part of this book focuses on what is called the 'extended police family' under the Police Reform Act 2002. For a number of reasons, this involves a slightly different concept to that covered in the first part. Although the second part describes the extended use of civilians in police duties, it is important to note that many will be subject to the direct control of the relevant chief officers of police. However, the statutory provisions concerning these designated and accredited civilians also contain many contentious points, which will be the subject of later discussion.

It is interesting to note that some designated or accredited civilians may come from the private security industry, which is a further example of this industry becoming increasingly involved in public protection duties. Many would argue that this blurs the distinction between private and public security even further. This assertion will be analysed in the second part of this book, although it will be some time before the full effects of these measures are finally known. Meanwhile, the current role of the private security industry, in public protection duties rather than purely commercial risk management, will now be discussed.

---

4   According to s 3 and Sched 2 to the Private Security Industry Act 2001.

PART I:
THE DEVOLUTION OF PUBLIC PROTECTION DUTIES TO THE PRIVATE SECURITY INDUSTRY

CHAPTER 1

AIRPORT SECURITY

In response to rising concerns regarding aviation security, the Protection of Aircraft Act 1973 was enacted. Part II of this Act, entitled 'Protection of Aircraft, Aerodromes and Air Navigation Installations against Acts of Violence', contained s 10 (repealed and subsequently expanded), which made the following provisions:

(1) For the purposes to which this Part of this Act applies the Secretary of State may give a direction in writing to the manager of any aerodrome in the United Kingdom requiring him to use his best endeavours to secure that such searches to which this section applies as are specified in the direction are carried out by constables or by *other persons*[1] of a description specified in the direction.

(2) The searches to which this section applies, in relation to an aerodrome, are searches –

   (a) of the aerodrome or any part of it;

   (b) of any aircraft which at the time is in any part of the aerodrome; and

   (c) of persons or property (other than aircraft) which may at any such time be in any part of the aerodrome.

It will be noted that the words 'other persons' have been emphasised. This provision caused some concern, as illustrated in an extract from a letter sent by Inspector Reg Gale to the Home Secretary on 2 September 1973, in which he states:

> When one takes personnel such as these who are not vetted,[2] selected or trained to the standards of a constable and who do not hold the office of constable, and places them in a situation where by law they have the right to detain and search members of the public, it must give cause for concern.[3]

The Protection of Aircraft Act was later repealed by the Aviation Security Act 1982, which under s 13 extended the powers of both the police and 'other persons' to search persons, property and vehicles, as well as aircraft. These provisions were extended yet further by a new s 13A, which was inserted by s 2 of the Aviation and Maritime Security Act 1990. Sections 13 and 13A of the Aviation Security Act 1982 are as follows:

13(1) For purposes to which this Part of this Act applies, the Secretary of State may give a direction in writing to the manager of any aerodrome in the United Kingdom requiring him to use his best endeavours to secure that such searches to which this section applies as are specified in the direction are

---

1   Emphasis added.
2   Measures were subsequently taken which strengthened the vetting of security staff at airports.
3   Quoted from the article published in *The Observer* by Draper, H, reproduced in *Private Police*, 1978, Penguin.

carried out by constables or by *other persons*[4] of a description specified in the direction.

(2) The searches to which this section applies, in relation to an aerodrome, are searches –

    (a) of the aerodrome or any part of it;

    (b) of any aircraft which at the time when the direction is given or at any subsequent time is in any part of the aerodrome; and

    (c) of persons or property (other than aircraft) which may at any such time be in any part of the aerodrome.

(3) Without prejudice to section 7(1) of this Act,[5] where a direction given under this section to the manager of an aerodrome is for the time being in force, then if a constable, or *any other person*[6] specified in the direction in accordance with this section, has reasonable cause to suspect that an article to which section 4 of this Act[7] applies is in, or may be brought into, any part of the aerodrome, he may, by virtue of this subsection and without a warrant, search any part of the aerodrome or any aircraft, vehicle, goods or other moveable property of any description which, or any person who, is for the time being in any part of the aerodrome, and for that purpose –

    (a) may enter any building or works in the aerodrome, or enter upon any land in the aerodrome, if need be by force; and

    (b) may stop any such aircraft, vehicle, goods, property or person and detain him for so long as may be necessary for that purpose.

(4) Any person who –

    (a) without reasonable excuse fails to comply with a direction given to him under this section; or

    (b) intentionally obstructs or impedes a person acting in the exercise of a power conferred on him by subsection (3) above,

shall be guilty of an offence and liable –

    (i) on summary conviction, to a fine not exceeding the statutory maximum;

    (ii) on conviction on indictment, to a fine or to imprisonment for a term not exceeding two years or to both.

13A(1) For purposes to which this Part of this Act applies, the Secretary of State may give a direction to any person (other than the manager of an aerodrome) who –

    (a) occupies any land forming part of an aerodrome in the United Kingdom; or

    (b) is permitted to have access to a restricted zone of such an aerodrome for the purposes of the activities of a business carried on by him, requiring him to use his best endeavours to secure that such searches to which this

---

4   Emphasis added.
5   This refers to the power of a constable to prevent a person from travelling on an aircraft who is suspected of intending to commit offences such as hijacking, destroying, damaging or endangering the safety of aircraft, or other acts likely to endanger aircraft safety.
6   Emphasis added.
7   Such articles include firearms (real or imitation), explosives or any offensive weapons.

section applies as are specified in the direction are carried out by constables or by *other persons*[8] of a description specified in the direction.

(2) The searches to which this section applies are –

  (a) in relation to a person falling within subsection (1)(a) above, searches –

    (i) of the land which he occupies within the aerodrome, and

    (ii) of persons or property which may at any time be on that land, and

  (b) in relation to a person falling within subsection (1)(b) above, searches –

    (i) of any land which he occupies outside the aerodrome for the purposes of his business, and

    (ii) of persons or property which may at any time be on that land.

(3) Any person who, without reasonable excuse, fails to comply with a direction given to him under this section shall be guilty of an offence and liable –

  (a) on summary conviction, to a fine not exceeding the statutory maximum;

  (b) on conviction on indictment, to a fine or to imprisonment not exceeding two years, or to both.

(4) Where a person is convicted of an offence under subsection (3) above, then, if without reasonable excuse the failure in respect of which he was convicted is continued after the conviction, he shall be guilty of a further offence and liable on summary conviction to a fine not exceeding one-tenth of level 5 on the standard scale for each day on which the failure continues.

Most recently, s 84 of the Anti-Terrorism, Crime and Security Act 2001 has enhanced the powers of the police and civilians under the amended ss 21C and 21D of the Aviation Security Act 1982. This will enable a constable, the manager of an aerodrome, or a person acting on his behalf, to use reasonable force to remove a person whose presence in a restricted zone or aircraft is unauthorised.

Despite what appears to be a comprehensive range of powers available to civilian security officers in airports, a number of gaps seem evident. For instance, no power of arrest is attached to the offences of intentionally obstructing or impeding such officers. Neither of them are arrestable offences under s 24 and Sched 1A of the Police and Criminal Evidence Act (PACE) 1984 (see Appendix 1 for the range of these offences) and, as they are not police officers, the general arrest conditions under s 25 of PACE are not available. These are powers available only to the police, which enable them to arrest persons under a number of conditions that are listed in Appendix 2. There is also only limited scope in using the common law power to arrest in order to deal with a breach of the peace. In any event, the arrest must be for an actual or apprehended breach of the peace and not for intentionally obstructing or impeding the officers in question. If a consequence of the obstruction involves an assault, occasioning actual bodily harm (or more serious injury) or criminal damage to the officer's uniform or other property, for instance, these could amount to arrestable offences.

Section 3(1) of the Criminal Law Act 1967 states that a person may use reasonable force to prevent crime, effect or assist in the lawful arrest of offenders or suspected offenders, or persons unlawfully at large. If there is no arrest power to begin with, persons cannot be *lawfully* arrested. In other words, s 3(1) does not confer a blanket power of arrest for every transgression against the criminal law. However, it is submitted that it may be used in a situation where, for example, a security officer is assaulted and the assailant makes, or is likely to make, a further attack on the officer or someone else. Reasonable force may then be used to *prevent* this crime, the offence being another assault, or even damage to property. The use of force in this instance could include restraining the person concerned until the police arrive to make the arrest. Before departing from the restrictions on the powers of airport security officers, it should also be noted that no express power of seizure appears to have been conferred upon these security operatives either.

Section 82 of the Anti-Terrorism, Crime and Security Act 2001, however, has created three new arrestable offences under s 24 and Sched 1A of PACE. These include two offences related to the power to use reasonable force to remove unauthorised persons from aircraft and prohibited zones, mentioned above, and also a power related to the Civil Aviation Act 1982. These offences are under ss 21C(1) and 21D(1) of the Aviation Security Act 1982 (unauthorised presence in a restricted zone or on an aircraft) and s 39(1) of the Civil Aviation Act 1982 (trespass on an aerodrome). By virtue of these offences being classed as arrestable, it confers the power of a citizen's arrest on non-police personnel, which can include airport security officers, of course.

Notwithstanding the anomalies mentioned above, the provision of the above powers exercisable by any 'other person' means that not only the police but also civilian security officers may be authorised to conduct the wide range of searches empowered under the Aviation Security Act 1982. It should be noted that civilian security operatives are included in other provisions under that Act. For example, the new s 20B enables an 'authorised person' to give a 'detention direction', preventing certain aircraft which are at risk from flying. Reasonable force may be used to enforce this measure by the authorised person or by another person acting under his authority. It is not surprising, therefore, that a substantial amount of routine airport security is in the hands of private security operatives. This is the first example of specific public protection duties being devolved to the private security sector. It also provides an illustration of statutory powers that are not held by conventional security officers being conferred upon specific private security operatives. This trend has been significantly extended through the relevant provisions under the Criminal Justice Act 1991, the Criminal Justice and Public Order Act 1994, the Immigration and Asylum Act 1999, the Channel Tunnel (Security) Order 1994 and the Access to Justice Act 1999. These will, in turn, be discussed in the next six chapters.

CHAPTER 2

MAGISTRATES' COURT SECURITY OFFICERS

The substitution of the police by civilian security officers in the magistrates' courts has been very apparent in recent years. The Le Vay Report[1] identified the need for a visible uniformed presence to replace the diminished high police profile that once existed in those courts. The reason for this general reduction in police numbers during magistrates' court proceedings is largely due to the way in which prosecutions are presented, especially since the 1980s, when the Crown Prosecution Service removed this responsibility from the police. Section 76 under Pt IV of the Criminal Justice Act 1991 makes provision for those responsible for maintaining the magistrates' courts to either directly appoint or contract-in security officers for the purpose of maintaining order. These security operatives have also been given statutory powers in pursuance of their duties and therefore are not restricted to ordinary citizens' powers applicable to conventional security officers. The powers and duties of magistrates' court security officers are to be found under s 77 of the 1991 Act as follows:

(1) A court security officer acting in the execution of his duty shall have the following powers, namely –

    (a) to search any person who is in or is seeking to enter the court-house, and any article in the possession of such a person;

    (b) to exclude or remove from the court-house any person who refuses to permit such a search as is mentioned in paragraph (a) above, or refuses to surrender any article in his possession which the officer reasonably believes may jeopardise the maintenance of order in the court-house;

    (c) to exclude or remove any person from the court-house, or restrain any person in the court-house, where (in either case) it is reasonably necessary to do so in order –

        (i) to maintain order in the court-house;

        (ii) to enable court business to be carried on without interference or delay; or

        (iii) to secure his or any other person's safety.

(2) The powers conferred by subsection (1)(a) above to search a person shall not be construed as authorising a court security officer to require a person to remove any of his clothing other than an outer coat, jacket or gloves.

(3) The powers conferred by subsection (1)(b) and (c) above shall include power to use reasonable force where necessary.

(4) In the execution of his duty, a court security officer shall act in accordance with any general or specific instructions which have been given to him (whether orally or in writing) by a person in authority.

(5) In subsection (4) above 'person in authority', in relation to any court-house, means –

    (a) a justice of the peace, justices' chief executive or justice's clerk who is exercising any functions in the court-house; and

---

1 *Magistrates' Courts: Report of a Scrutiny*, 1989, HMSO.

    (b) any officer or staff of the magistrates' courts committee authorised by such a justices' chief executive or clerk for the purpose.

    (6) For the purposes of this section and section 78 below, a court security officer shall not be regarded as acting in the execution of his duty at any time when he is not readily identifiable as such an officer (whether by means of a uniform or badge which he is wearing or otherwise).

The bulk of these powers appear to be very similar to those held by the police, particularly where they relate to the searching of members of the public. However, note that reasonable suspicion is not required before a search can be exercised and there is no requirement for many of the general procedures under PACE to be complied with. The latter may be due to the fact that magistrates' court security officers should wear name badges when on duty (or wear a uniform, or preferably both) and, in contrast to police search powers, there is no provision for reasonable force to be used to carry out a search. Force may only be used in order to exclude or restrain persons causing disruption or likely to cause danger, or where persons refuse to be searched or surrender any article in their possession.

    There is the question of whether the search powers of these security officers (and others mentioned in this book) could be challenged under the Human Rights Act 1998. As these powers may be exercised without any prerequisite reasonable suspicion, could this constitute a breach of Art 5(1)(c) of the European Convention on Human Rights? This prohibits the deprivation of a person's liberty unless, *inter alia*, it is reasonably considered necessary to prevent an offence being committed. It could be argued that searches by magistrates' court security officers are meant to prevent crime and, as force should not be used in their execution, there may not be a breach of the Convention. It is also submitted that in some instances, these searches could be construed as a condition of entry or remaining on the premises, rather than a significant intrusion of a person's liberty.

    Provision is made for the protection of magistrates' court security officers by creating specific offences against those who assault, resist or wilfully obstruct them. These offences have been created under s 78 of the 1991 Act as follows:

    (1) Any person who assaults a court security officer acting in the execution of his duty shall be liable on summary conviction to a fine not exceeding level 5 on the standard scale[2] or to imprisonment for a term not exceeding six months or to both.

    (2) Any person who resists or wilfully obstructs a court security officer acting in the execution of his duty shall be liable on summary conviction to a fine not exceeding level 3[3] on the standard scale.

At first sight, the maximum penalties seem identical with those under s 89 of the Police Act 1996, except that wilfully obstructing police may also carry a maximum of one month's imprisonment, as well as a fine not exceeding level 3 on the standard scale. There also appear to be some gaps in the powers of magistrates' court security officers (and others discussed in this book). For

---

2   Currently £5,000.
3   Currently £1,000.

instance, if a person assaults a court security officer, under what power can that officer effect an arrest? If the assailant causes or is reasonably suspected of having inflicted actual bodily harm or worse, such offences are arrestable under s 24 and Sched 1A of PACE; therefore, this power is generally available to non-police officers. Supposing the offence is merely a common assault, though, as it appears to be under s 78(1) of the 1991 Act; this is not an arrestable offence, so how can the assailant be brought to justice?

Police officers may rely on the general arrest conditions under s 25 of PACE, but this is not available to court security officers. It appears that one possibility could be an arrest under the common law power to deal with or prevent a breach of the peace. However, a breach of the peace has a rather fluid definition and is interpreted at the discretion of magistrates in individual cases. The position becomes even less certain in instances where court security officers are resisted or wilfully obstructed. As such offences do not necessarily involve violence or even the threat of violence, the power to deal with a breach of the peace may not be relied on in such cases. As mentioned above, when discussing similar limitations on security officers at the airports, the arrest would have to be for an actual or apprehended breach of the peace and not an assault or wilful obstruction.

A further problem may exist due to the absence of an express power of seizure. The wording under the 1991 Act confers a power to require certain classes of articles to be surrendered which, it is reasonably believed, may jeopardise order in the court-house. But this is only a temporary deprivation of an article and not outright seizure. What would happen, for instance, if court security officers discovered evidence of a crime during a search? This problem is likely to exist until proposed reforms under the Courts Bill become law. This will be discussed below.

It should be noted that these powers are applicable to security officers working in the magistrates' courts only. Ironically, security officers permanently employed in other courts have not been given these powers and therefore are restricted to ordinary citizens' powers. In other words, security officers employed in the Crown Court, for instance, have no more powers than a conventional security officer working in a supermarket.[4] This anomaly was identified by Auld LJ in his review of the criminal courts, where he stated:

> Curiously, they have less powers in the Crown Court than in magistrates' courts. In the Crown Court they have no powers to search, eject, control or restrain persons in the building ... [they cannot] ... forcibly search or arrest anyone causing trouble inside the building.[5]

This anomaly is due to be rectified under the Courts Bill, which was introduced in the House of Lords on 28 November 2002. The provisions of this Bill, as originally published, are as follows:

---

4 For a more detailed analysis of this issue, see Jason-Lloyd, L, 'Security in the courts' (2002) 166(15) Justice of the Peace, pp 280–83.
5 Auld, R (Sir), *Review of the Criminal Courts*, October 2001, The Stationery Office.

PART 4

COURT SECURITY

46 Court security officers

(1) A court security officer is a person who is –

   (a) appointed by the Lord Chancellor under section 2(1) or provided under arrangements made by him under section 2(4), and

   (b) designated by the Lord Chancellor as a court security officer.

(2) The Lord Chancellor may by regulations make provision as to –

   (a) training courses to be completed by court security officers,

   (b) conditions to be met before a person may be designated as a court security officer.

(3) For the purposes of this Part a court security officer who is not readily identifiable as such (whether by means of his uniform or badge or otherwise) is not to be regarded as acting in the execution of his duty.

47 Powers of search

(1) A court security officer acting in the execution of his duty may search –

   (a) any person who is in, or seeking to enter, a court building, and

   (b) any article in the possession of such a person.

(2) Subsection (1) does not authorise the officer to require a person to remove any of his clothing other than a coat, jacket, gloves or hat.

(3) In this Part 'court building' means any building –

   (a) where the business of any of the courts referred to in section 1 is carried on, and

   (b) to which the public has access.

48 Powers to exclude, remove or restrain persons

(1) A court security officer acting in the execution of his duty may exclude or remove from a court building, or a part of a court building, any person who refuses –

   (a) to permit a search under section 47(1), or

   (b) to surrender an article in his possession when asked to do so under section 49(1).

(2) A court security officer acting in the execution of his duty may –

   (a) restrain any person who is in a court building, or

   (b) exclude or remove any person from a court building, or part of a court building,

   if it is reasonably necessary to do so for one of the purposes given in subsection (3).

(3) The purposes are –

   (a) enabling court business to be carried on without interference or delay;

   (b) maintaining order;

   (c) securing the safety of any person in the court building.

(4) A court security officer acting in the execution of his duty may remove any person from a courtroom at the request of a judge or a justice of the peace.

(5) The powers conferred by subsections (1), (2) and (4) include the power to use reasonable force, where necessary.

49 Surrender and seizure of articles

(1) If a court security officer acting in the execution of his duty reasonably believes that an article in the possession of a person who is in, or seeking to enter, a court building, ought to be surrendered on any of the grounds given in subsection (3), he must ask the person to surrender the article.

(2) If the person refuses to surrender the article, the officer may seize it.

(3) The grounds are that the article –

    (a) may jeopardise the maintenance of order in the court building (or a part of it);

    (b) may put the safety of any person in the court building at risk, or

    (c) may be evidence of, or in relation to, an offence.

50 Powers to retain articles surrendered or seized

(1) Subject to subsection (2), a court security officer may retain an article which was –

    (a) surrendered in response to a request under section 49(1), or

    (b) seized under section 49(2),

until the time when the person who surrendered it, from whom it was seized, is leaving the court building.

(2) If a court security officer reasonably believes that the article may be evidence of, or in relation to, an offence, he may retain it until –

    (a) the time when the person who surrendered it, or from whom it was seized, is leaving the court building, or

    (b) the end of the permitted period,

whichever is later.

(3) 'The permitted period' means such period, not exceeding 24 hours from the time the article was surrendered or seized, as will enable the court security officer to draw the article to the attention of a constable.

51 Regulations about retention of articles

(1) The Lord Chancellor may by regulations make provision as to –

    (a) the provision to persons –

        (i) by whom articles have been surrendered in response to a request under section 49(1); or

        (ii) from whom articles have been seized under section 49(2),

of written information about the powers of retention of court security officers,

    (b) the keeping of records about articles which have been so surrendered or seized,

    (c) the period for which unclaimed articles have been kept, and

    (d) the disposal of unclaimed articles at the end of that period.

(2) 'Unclaimed article' means an article –

    (a) which has been retained under section 50,

    (b) which a person is entitled to have returned to him,

(c) which has not been returned, and

(d) whose return has not been requested by a person entitled to it.

52 Assaulting and obstructing court security officers

(1) Any person who assaults a court security officer acting in the execution of his duty commits an offence.

(2) A person guilty of an offence under subsection (1) is liable on summary conviction to –

(a) a fine not exceeding level 5 on the standard scale, or

(b) imprisonment for a term not exceeding six months,

or to both.

(3) A person who resists or wilfully obstructs a court security officer acting in the execution of his duty commits an offence.

(4) A person guilty of an offence under subsection (3) is liable on summary conviction to a fine not exceeding level 3 on the standard scale.

An examination of Pt 4 of the Courts Bill discloses a number of differences between its provisions and those that currently exist. One of the most obvious is that there will be a single class of security officer for all the courts, with equal powers and duties. No longer will special powers be conferred only on security officers in the magistrates' courts. Another difference is that whereas the latter may only request the surrender of an article reasonably believed to cause danger or disruption, in future, all security officers in the courts will be empowered to seize an article if this request is refused. Furthermore, an article that is reasonably believed to constitute evidence of a crime or be related to a criminal offence may be seized under these powers. Such articles may then be retained for up to 24 hours, in order to be brought to the attention of the police. Other differences include the power to remove hats, currently excluded from the ambit of the present search powers, and that a 'coat' may be removed during a search rather than an 'outer coat'.

An important point regarding these proposed changes is that no specific powers of arrest are being conferred upon court security officers. This is made clear in the explanatory notes to the Courts Bill, which state:

> No new or statutory powers of arrest are conferred on court security officers. Court security officers will, like all citizens, have power to make an arrest under section 24 of the Police and Criminal Evidence Act 1984 and the common law. Section 24 provides that 'any person' may arrest without a warrant anyone who is committing or who he has reasonable grounds to suspect is committing an arrestable offence. Criminal Law Act 1967, section 3 confers a power on a person to use such force as is reasonable in the circumstances in the prevention of crime or in effecting or assisting in the lawful arrest of offenders or suspected offenders.

Notwithstanding the above statement regarding arrest powers, it is submitted that the lack of specific powers for court security officers to arrest where they are assaulted, resisted or wilfully obstructed can still leave them in a vulnerable position. As argued above and in later chapters, s 24 of PACE is limited to arrestable offences only. None of the specific offences against these civilian security operatives are arrestable. Section 3(1) of the Criminal Law Act 1967 only applies to the use of reasonable force to *lawfully* arrest persons. If there is no power of arrest to begin with, how can the arrest be lawful? Also, the use of force to prevent crime under s 3(1) mainly applies to self-defence or the defence of others or property; it does not confer a blanket arrest power for every offence. As mentioned above under airport security, it might be used to justify restraining a person who has already committed or is likely to commit an offence. In any event, the degree of force used must be proportionate and justifiable in the light of the harm being prevented.

The common law power to deal with, or prevent, a breach of the peace is mainly confined to violence or anticipated violence (see *R v Howell* [1981] 3 All ER 383; [1982] QB 416 and *R v Kelbie* [1996] Crim LR 802), although it may be used in defence of property in certain circumstances. Where there is an actual or threatened breach, the law permits a citizen to take action which falls short of making an arrest. This can involve temporarily restraining and detaining the person to enable him to calm down (see *Albert v Lavin* [1982] AC 546; [1981] 1 All ER 628). Resisting or wilfully obstructing a court security officer (or other civilian security operative, as will be discussed later) may not involve violence, so how can the common law power apply? Even if it is used in assault cases, the arrest must be for an actual or anticipated breach of the peace, and not for the specific offence of assaulting a court security officer. As mentioned above, a more serious assault, such as occasioning actual bodily harm or even grievous bodily harm, would constitute an arrestable offence. Also, if an arrestable offence were committed, such as criminal damage, as well as a common assault on the security officer, the situation may well be different.

Recent research has shown that a two-tier security system currently operates at one Crown Court, and this is quite possibly the case at others. The main reception area is the responsibility of ordinary security officers, whereas the security of the court building, where prisoners are held or are in transit, is under the control of prisoner custody officers. This category of security operatives is the next to be discussed as they are also from the private security sector and have been given special powers under statute.

CHAPTER 3

PRISONER CUSTODY OFFICERS

Part IV of the Criminal Justice Act 1991 went much further than giving special powers to magistrates' court security officers. It created further classes of private security operatives engaged in public protection duties and gave them specific powers accordingly. Sections 80–86 and Sched 10 of the 1991 Act collectively cover the provision, monitoring, certification and powers and duties of prisoner custody officers. There are two classes of prisoner custody officers, namely those working in the prisoner escort service and those responsible for front-line security in the privately-managed prisons. In some cases, these personnel may be trained to perform both functions.

The responsibility for the security arrangements of prisoners in transit was systematically removed from the police and the prison service during the early 1990s.[1] The government at that time sought to find a more cost-effective system rather than continuing to rely on police and prison officers, which proved to be a substantial drain on the manpower of both services. Section 80 of the Criminal Justice Act 1991 empowers the Home Secretary to contract out the escort and transport arrangements for prisoners going to and from places such as the courts, police stations and prisons. Those responsible for transporting and guarding prisoners in this capacity are called prisoner custody officers, whose powers and duties are provided under s 82 of the 1991 Act as follows:

(1) A prisoner custody officer acting in pursuance of prisoner escort arrangements shall have the following powers, namely –

   (a) to search in accordance with rules made by the Secretary of State any prisoner for whose delivery or custody he is responsible in pursuance of the arrangements; and

   (b) to search any other person who is in or is seeking to enter any place where any such prisoner is or is to be held, and any article in the possession of such a person.

(2) The powers conferred by subsection (1)(b) above to search a person shall not be construed as authorising a prisoner custody officer to require a person to remove any of his clothing other than an outer coat, jacket or gloves.

(3) A prisoner custody officer shall have the following duties as respects prisoners for whose delivery or custody he is responsible in pursuance of prisoner escort arrangements, namely –

   (a) to prevent their escape from lawful custody;

   (b) to prevent, or detect and report on, the commission or attempted commission by them of other unlawful acts;

   (c) to ensure good order and discipline on their part;

   (d) to attend to their wellbeing; and

   (e) to give effect to any directions as to their treatment which are given by a court,

---

1   With the exception of Category 'A' prisoners.

and the Secretary of State may make rules with respect to the performance by prisoner custody officers of their duty under paragraph (d) above.

(4) Where a prisoner custody officer acting in pursuance of prisoner escort arrangements is on any premises in which the Crown Court or a magistrates' court is sitting, it shall be his duty to give effect to any order of that court made –

   (a) in the case of the Crown Court, under section 142 of the Powers of Criminal Courts (Sentencing) Act 2000 (power of Court to order search of persons before it); or

   (b) in the case of a magistrates' court, under section 80 of the 1980 Act (application of money found on defaulter).

(5) The powers conferred by subsection (1) above, and the powers arising by virtue of subsections (3) and (4) above, shall include power to use reasonable force where necessary.

(6) The power to make rules under this section shall be exercisable by statutory instrument which shall be subject to annulment in pursuance of a resolution of either House of Parliament.

Prisoner custody officers working in the privately-managed prisons have their powers and duties defined under s 86 of the 1991 Act, which will be reproduced and discussed below. At this point, it may be useful to mention the context within which privately-managed prisons exist at the present time. There are two aspects to this scheme. First, there are prisons that are State-owned but whose management is vested in an approved company that is given a contract to run the relevant penal establishment. Secondly, there are prisons that are completely privatised, meaning that approved companies have been contracted to design, construct, manage and finance them. The companies that are currently involved in privately-managing the relevant prisons include Group 4 Prison Services, Premier Custodial Group, Securicor Custodial Services and UK Detention Services. Section 86 of the 1991 Act defines the powers and duties of prisoner custody officers working in these prisons as follows:

(1) A prisoner custody officer performing custodial duties at a contracted-out prison shall have the following powers, namely –

   (a) to search in accordance with prison rules any prisoner who is confined in the prison; and

   (b) to search any other person who is in or is seeking to enter the prison, and any article in the possession of such a person.

(2) The powers conferred by subsection 1(b) above to search a person shall not be construed as authorising a prisoner custody officer to require a person to remove any of his clothing other than an outer coat, jacket or gloves.

(3) A prisoner custody officer performing custodial duties at a contracted-out prison shall have the following duties as respects prisoners confined in the prison, namely –

   (a) to prevent their escape from lawful custody;

   (b) to prevent, or detect and report on, the commission or attempted commission by them of other unlawful acts;

   (c) to ensure good order and discipline on their part; and

   (d) to attend to their wellbeing.

(4) The powers conferred by subsection (1) above, and the powers arising by virtue of subsection (3) above, shall include power to use reasonable force where necessary.

A fundamental difference between the search powers of prisoner custody officers and magistrates' court security officers is that the former have the power to use reasonable force where necessary in the exercise of these powers. This applies to the searching of non-prisoners as well as prisoners. Both classes of prisoner custody officers, whether working in the prisoner escort service or in privately-managed prisons, are subject to the provisions under s 90 of the 1991 Act with regard to their protection. These provisions are almost identical to those applicable to magistrates' court security officers in respect of assault, resistance and wilful obstruction. The maximum penalties on conviction are the same, although in the case of prisoner custody officers, a further offence is included, namely possession of a real or imitation firearm during an assault. This is punishable by a maximum of life imprisonment. These protective measures are as follows, but note that only prisoner custody officers on escort duties are required to wear a badge or uniform in order to fall within the ambit of s 90:

Protection of prisoner custody officers

(1) Any person who assaults a prisoner custody officer –

    (a) acting in pursuance of prisoner escort arrangements;

    (b) performing custodial duties at a contracted-out prison; or

    (c) performing contracted-out functions at a directly managed prison,

    shall be liable on summary conviction to a fine not exceeding level 5 on the standard scale or to imprisonment for a term not exceeding six months or to both.

(2) Section 17(2) of the Firearms Act 1968 (additional penalty for possession of firearms when committing certain offences) shall apply to offences under subsection (1) above.

(3) Any person who resists or wilfully obstructs a prisoner custody officer –

    (a) acting in pursuance of prisoner escort arrangements;

    (b) performing custodial duties at a contracted-out prison; or

    (c) performing contracted-out functions at a directly managed prison,

    shall be liable on summary conviction to a fine not exceeding level 3 on the standard scale.

(4) For the purposes of this section, a prisoner custody officer shall not be regarded as acting in pursuance of prisoner escort arrangements at any time when he is not readily identifiable as such an officer (whether by means of a uniform or badge which he is wearing or otherwise).

Several of the anomalies apparent under the protective measures applicable to magistrates' court security officers also seem to apply to prisoner custody officers. If any of the latter is assaulted by a member of the public, what is the power under which the assailant can be arrested? Again, it appears that there is no power to arrest the assailant in order to have that person prosecuted, unless it is an aggravated assault causing actual bodily harm (or where a firearm is in evidence). The limitations regarding arrests under s 3(1) of the Criminal Law

Act 1967, as mentioned above regarding civilian airport security operatives, would seem to apply to prisoner custody officers. The common-law power to arrest for a breach of the peace would not always be applicable here, especially with regard to the offences of resistance and wilful obstruction. In any event, the arrest will be for a breach of the peace and not for any of the specific offences under s 90. Also, no express power of seizure appears to have been conferred upon prisoner custody officers when searching non-prisoners. These omissions are not relevant to prisoners, because they are under lawful detention.

Prison officers appointed by HM Prison Service are not faced with this problem. Section 8 of the Prison Act 1952 states that they have the full powers of a constable in the course of their duties as prison officers; therefore, they have access to the vast array of powers available to the police. According to the wording of s 87(3) of the Criminal Justice Act 1991, this does not apply to prisoner custody officers employed in the privately-managed prisons, although, curiously, there is no express preclusion of this from the powers held by prisoner custody officers in the escort service. This seems particularly odd, as prisoner custody officers can be double-trained and authorised to perform both functions.

It is important to mention another distinction between prisoner custody officers in the private sector and prison officers in HM Prison Service. Prisoner custody officers, as well as other employees, such as ancillary staff in the prisoner escort service or the privately-managed prisons, are subject to s 91 of the Criminal Justice Act 1991. This is designed to ensure confidentiality in the course of their employment and afterwards. Section 91 creates the following triable either-way offence as follows:

Wrongful disclosure of information

(1) A person who –

   (a) is or has been employed (whether as a prisoner custody officer or otherwise) in pursuance of prisoner escort arrangements, or at a contracted-out prison; or

   (b) is or has been employed to perform contracted-out functions at a directly managed prison,

   shall be guilty of an offence if he discloses, otherwise than in the course of his duty or as authorised by the Secretary of State, any information which he acquired in the course of his employment and which relates to a particular prisoner.

(2) A person guilty of an offence under subsection (1) above shall be liable –

   (a) on conviction on indictment, to imprisonment for a term not exceeding two years or a fine or both;

   (b) on summary conviction, to imprisonment for a term not exceeding six months or a fine not exceeding the statutory maximum or both.

Sections 97 and 99 of the Criminal Justice and Public Order Act 1994 enable an interchange between prisoner custody officers and prison officers. In appropriate circumstances, therefore, it is possible for prisoner custody officers to be seconded to State prisons and prison officers to be seconded to privately-managed prisons. Although this would obviously apply to emergency situations, longer term arrangements may also be made under these provisions.

However, when prisoner custody officers are seconded to State penal establishments, they are still excluded from the ambit of s 8 of the Prison Act 1952 and therefore do not have the status of a constable when on duty.

The certification of all prisoner custody officers, which authorises them to be employed in that capacity, is subject to the provisions of Sched 10 to the Criminal Justice Act 1991. This includes, *inter alia*, the provisions governing the suspension and revocation of certificates, as well as creating a summary offence under para 5 of Sched 10 as follows:

> 5   If any person, for the purpose of obtaining a certificate for himself or for another person –
>
> (a) makes a statement which he knows to be false in a material particular; or
>
> (b) recklessly makes a statement which is false in a material particular,
>
> he shall be liable on summary conviction to a fine not exceeding level 4 on the standard scale.[2]

In order for a prisoner custody officer to receive a certificate, such a person must satisfy the requirement that he is a fit and proper person to hold such office, as well as having received appropriate training.

Finally, brief mention will be made of the mechanisms for the supervision and general accountability of prisoner custody officers. Under s 85 of the Criminal Justice Act 1991, the general functioning of a privately-managed prison is the responsibility of the director, who is overseen by a Crown servant known as the controller. It is also the responsibility of the latter to investigate complaints against prisoner custody officers. With regard to the prisoner escort service, s 81 of the Criminal Justice Act 1991 makes provision for the appointment of a prisoner escort monitor. This Crown servant is responsible for keeping the escort arrangements under review and for investigating allegations of discipline offences by prisoners, as well as complaints against prisoner custody officers. Section 81 also makes provision for the appointment of a panel of lay observers, who are under a duty to inspect the conditions under which prisoners are held.

---

2   Currently £2,500.

CHAPTER 4

CUSTODY OFFICERS (SECURE TRAINING CENTRES)

The custody officers to be discussed here should not be confused with the custody officers under PACE 1984. The latter are police officers, usually of the rank of sergeant, who are primarily responsible for ensuring the proper treatment of detained suspects, as well as maintaining correct procedures applicable to the custody suites at police stations. Those referred to in this chapter are custody officers created under Pt I of the Criminal Justice and Public Order Act 1994.

This Part of the 1994 Act made important provisions regarding young offenders and, *inter alia*, instituted a new custodial regime for offenders aged between 12 and 14. These are called secure training centres and, currently, three such institutions are operational, with the possibility of three more at some future stage. Originally, these institutions were intended to accommodate up to 40 trainees within the age groups mentioned above. However, since the inclusion of secure training centres under the auspices of detention and training orders, originally under the Crime and Disorder Act 1998,[1] these centres now accommodate a higher number of young offenders and some are aged up to 17. The maximum period of actual detention within a secure training centre is about one year, subject to variable early release provisions.[2]

All secure training centres are privately managed and have a very similar command structure to the adult penal institutions in terms of daily management and overall accountability. Those responsible for the front-line security and maintenance of order within the secure training centres are called custody officers. Under s 9 of the Criminal Justice and Public Order Act 1994, their powers and duties are almost identical to those held by prisoner custody officers, the main exception being the inclusion of the power to remove headgear as well as outer coats, jackets or gloves when searching non-inmates. The power to remove headgear is not available to prisoner custody officers when searching non-prisoners in the course of custodial (or escort) duties:[3]

Powers and duties of custody officers employed at contracted out secure training centres

9(1)A custody officer performing custodial duties at a contracted out secure training centre shall have the following powers, namely –

(a) to search in accordance with secure training centre rules any offender who is detained in the secure training centre; and

---

1   Now consolidated under ss 100–07 of the Powers of Criminal Courts (Sentencing) Act 2000.

2   Under ss 100–07 of the Powers of Criminal Courts (Sentencing) Act 2000, the maximum term that may be imposed under a detention and training order is two years, although early release under supervision occurs either at, or about, the halfway stage. Depending on directions from the Secretary of State, early release can be up to two months before or after the halfway stage of the total sentence.

3   Magistrates' court security officers only have the power to require the removal of outer coat, jacket or gloves. This is in line with the general power of stop and search under PACE.

(b) to search any other person who is in or who is seeking to enter the secure training centre, and any article in the possession of such a person.

(2) The powers conferred by subsection (1)(b) above to search a person shall not be construed as authorising a custody officer to require a person to remove any of his clothing other than an outer coat, headgear, jacket or gloves.

(3) A custody officer performing custodial duties at a contracted out secure training centre shall have the following duties as respects offenders detained in the secure training centre, namely –

(a) to prevent their escape from lawful custody;

(b) to prevent, or detect and report on, the commission or attempted commission by them of other unlawful acts;

(c) to ensure good order and discipline on their part; and

(d) to attend to their wellbeing.

(4) The powers conferred by subsection (1) above, and the powers arising by virtue of subsection (3) above, shall include power to use reasonable force where necessary.

Under Sched 1 to the 1994 Act, secure training centres are subject to their own escort arrangements, for which the front-line operatives are also custody officers. Their powers and duties are almost the same as prisoner custody officers, although they have the additional power to remove headgear, as mentioned earlier. The relevant provisions of Sched 1 are as follows:

Powers and duties of custody officers acting in pursuance of escort arrangements

3(1) A custody officer acting in pursuance of escort arrangements shall have the following powers, namely –

(a) to search in accordance with rules made by the Secretary of State any offender for whose delivery or custody he is responsible in pursuance of the arrangements; and

(b) to search any other person who is in or is seeking to enter any place where any such offender is or is to be held, and any article in the possession of such a person.

(2) The powers conferred by sub-paragraph (1)(b) above to search a person shall not be construed as authorising a custody officer to require a person to remove any of his clothing other than an outer coat, headgear, jacket or gloves.

(3) A custody officer shall have the following duties as respects offenders for whose delivery or custody he is responsible in pursuance of escort arrangements, namely –

(a) to prevent their escape from lawful custody;

(b) to prevent, or detect and report on, the commission or attempted commission by them of other unlawful acts;

(c) to ensure good order and discipline on their part;

(d) to attend to their wellbeing; and

(e) to give effect to any directions as to their treatment which are given by a court,

and the Secretary of State may make rules with respect to the performance by custody officers of their duty under (d) above.

(4) The powers conferred by sub-paragraph (1) above, and the powers arising by virtue of sub-paragraph (3) above, shall include power to use reasonable force where necessary.

(5) The power to make rules under this paragraph shall be exercisable by statutory instrument which shall be subject to annulment in pursuance of a resolution of either House of Parliament.

Under s 13 of the 1994 Act, identical criminal sanctions apply to those who assault, resist or wilfully obstruct custody officers engaged in escort or custodial duties as to those offences committed against both classes of prisoner custody officers. There is also a replication of the offence under s 90(2) of the Criminal Justice Act 1991 as applied to prisoner custody officers, namely, possession of a real or imitation firearm during an assault. In the case of custody officers in the secure training centres, this protection also stems from s 17(2) and Sched 1 of the Firearms Act 1968. There are also the same apparent anomalies regarding the arrest of those who commit the offences of assault, resisting or wilfully obstructing (apart from those instances where the firearm offence is involved). Under what power, if any, can those who commit these offences be lawfully apprehended and ultimately brought to justice?:

Protection of custody officers at secure training centres

13(1) Any person who assaults a custody officer –

(a) acting in pursuance of escort arrangements;

(b) performing custodial duties at a contracted out secure training centre; or

(c) performing contracted out functions at a directly managed secure training centre,

shall be liable on summary conviction to a fine not exceeding level 5 on the standard scale or to imprisonment for a term not exceeding six months or to both.

(2) Any person who resists or wilfully obstructs a custody officer –

(a) acting in pursuance of escort arrangements;

(b) performing custodial duties at a contracted out secure training centre; or

(c) performing contracted out functions at a directly managed secure training centre,

shall be liable on summary conviction to a fine not exceeding level 3 on the standard scale.

(3) For the purposes of this section, a custody officer shall not be regarded as acting in pursuance of escort arrangements at any time when he is not readily identifiable as such an officer (whether by means of a uniform or badge which he is wearing or otherwise).

Section 14 of the Criminal Justice and Public Order Act 1994 makes provisions regarding 'Wrongful disclosure of information relating to offenders detained at secure training centres'. These are identical to s 91 of the Criminal Justice Act 1991, which applies to prisoner custody officers. Any person employed at a secure training centre, or ex-employee, whether a custody officer or ancillary member of staff, will commit an offence in the event of unauthorised disclosure of information about a particular offender. The same maximum penalties apply on conviction for this offence as those under s 91 of the 1991 Act, namely, a term of imprisonment not exceeding two years and/or a fine when tried on indictment; or, if tried summarily, a maximum of six months' imprisonment and/or a fine not exceeding the statutory maximum.

The certification of custody officers in the secure training centres, and those who are part of their escort arrangements, must occur before they can be appointed. As mentioned above, this also applies to prisoner custody officers. All such officers must satisfy the requirement that they are fit and proper persons to hold such office and must receive training to the appropriate standard. It is an offence for anyone who, for the purpose of obtaining a certificate for himself or another person, makes a false or reckless statement. This is punishable by a fine not exceeding level 4 on the standard scale. The provisions regarding the issue, suspension and revocation of these certificates are to be found under Sched 2 to the Criminal Justice and Public Order Act 1994.

Custody officers are subject to the same basic framework of supervision and accountability as prisoner custody officers. Under s 8 of the Criminal Justice and Public Order Act 1994, secure training centres are under the daily control and supervision of a director who, in turn, is overseen by a Crown servant known as a monitor (in the privately-managed prisons, they are known as controllers). The monitor is also responsible for investigating complaints against custody officers. Paragraph 2 of Sched 1 to the 1994 Act makes provision for the monitoring of the escort arrangements. This enables the appointment of a Crown servant to function as an escort monitor, who is responsible for keeping the escort arrangements under review and investigating complaints against custody officers. Lay observers are also appointed to inspect the conditions under which offenders are transported or held.

It will be observed that some of the above statutory provisions refer to directly-managed secure training centres. Although all such centres are privately-managed, the Conservative government which passed the Criminal Justice and Public Order Act 1994 wished to have the option of directly managing them, should the necessity arise. However, it is intended that all secure training centres within the current programme should be privately-managed; therefore, their direct management on a permanent basis seems increasingly unlikely.

CHAPTER 5

IMMIGRATION REMOVAL CENTRES

The trend of privatising or contracting out public protection functions to the private security sector was taken yet further under Pt VIII of the Immigration and Asylum Act 1999, as amended by the Nationality, Immigration and Asylum Act 2002. These provisions concern the private, and direct, management of places of detention for immigration detainees, which were previously governed by delegated legislation under Sched 2 to the Immigration Act 1971. This has now been placed on a full statutory footing, which significantly reflects the relevant measures under the Criminal Justice Act 1991 and the Criminal Justice and Public Order Act 1994.

Under the 1999 Act (as amended by s 66 of the Nationality, Immigration and Asylum Act 2002), there are two categories of places for the detention of immigration detainees. These are called immigration removal centres (formerly immigration detention centres) and short-term holding centres; those mainly responsible for the custodial and escort functions are called detainee custody officers. The reason for the use of the word 'mainly' is that ss 150(1)(b) and 154(5) of the Immigration and Asylum Act 1999 enable prisoner custody officers to exercise custodial duties at both these institutions, while prison officers are empowered to perform custodial duties only at the removal centres (although the Secretary of State has the power to extend the scope of their duties, as well as those of prisoner custody officers). The statutory provisions in respect of security personnel at the immigration removal centres (and at the short-term holding facilities) are reproduced as follows:

Contracted out functions at directly managed removal centres

150(1)   The Secretary of State may enter into a contract with another person –

    (a) for functions at, or connected with, a directly managed removal centre to be performed by detainee custody officers provided by that person; or

    (b) for such functions to be performed by certified prisoner custody officers who are provided by that person.

    (2) For the purposes of this section 'removal centre' includes a short-term holding facility.

Detainee custody officers

154(1)   On an application made to him under this section, the Secretary of State may certify that the applicant –

    (a) is authorised to perform escort functions; or

    (b) is authorised to perform both escort functions and custodial functions.

    (2) The Secretary of State may not issue a certificate of authorisation unless he is satisfied that the applicant –

    (a) is a fit and proper person to perform the functions to be authorised; and

    (b) has received training to such standard as the Secretary of State considers appropriate for the performance of those functions.

(3) A certificate of authorisation continues in force until such date, or the occurrence of such an event, as may be specified in the certificate but may be suspended or revoked under paragraph 7 of Schedule 11.

(4) A certificate which authorises the performance of both escort functions and custodial functions may specify one date or event for one of those functions and a different date or event for the other.

(5) The Secretary of State may confer functions of detainee custody officers on prison officers or prisoner custody officers.

(6) A prison officer acting under arrangements made under subsection (5) has all the powers, authority, protection and privileges of a constable.

(7) Schedule 11 makes further provision about detainee custody officers.

SCHEDULE 11
DETAINEE CUSTODY OFFICERS

Obtaining certificates of authorisation by false pretences

1   A person who, for the purpose of obtaining a certificate of authorisation for himself or for any other person –

    (a) makes a statement which he knows to be false in a material particular; or

    (b) recklessly makes a statement which is false in a material particular,

is guilty of an offence and liable on summary conviction to a fine not exceeding level 4 on the standard scale.

Powers and duties of detainee custody officers

2(1) A detainee custody officer exercising custodial functions has power –

    (a) to search (in accordance with rules made by the Secretary of State) any detained person in relation to whom the officer is exercising custodial functions; and

    (b) to search any other person who is in, or is seeking to enter, any place where any such detained person is or is to be held, and any article in the possession of such a person.

(2) The power conferred by sub-paragraph (1)(b) does not authorise requiring a person to remove any of his clothing other than an outer coat, jacket or glove.

(3) As respects a detained person in relation to whom he is exercising custodial functions, it is the duty of a detainee custody officer –

    (a) to prevent that person's escape from lawful custody;

    (b) to prevent, or detect and report on, the commission or attempted commission by him of other unlawful acts;

    (c) to ensure good order and discipline on his part; and

    (d) to attend to his wellbeing.

(4) The powers conferred by sub-paragraph (1), and the powers arising by virtue of sub-paragraph (3), include power to use reasonable force where necessary.

Short-term holding facilities

3(1) A detainee custody officer may perform functions of a custodial nature at a short-term holding facility (whether or not he is authorised to perform custodial functions at a removal centre).

(2) When doing so, he is to have the same powers and duties in relation to the facility and persons detained there as he would have if the facility were a removal centre.

Assaulting a detainee custody officer

4   A person who assaults a detainee custody officer who is –

   (a) acting in accordance with escort arrangements;

   (b) performing custodial functions; or

   (c) performing functions of a custodial nature at a short-term holding facility,

   is guilty of an offence and liable on summary conviction to a fine not exceeding level 5 on the standard scale or to imprisonment for a term not exceeding six months or to both.

Obstructing detainee custody officers

5   A person who resists or wilfully obstructs a detainee custody officer who is –

   (a) acting in accordance with escort arrangements;

   (b) performing custodial functions; or

   (c) performing functions of a custodial nature at a short-term holding facility,

   is guilty of an offence and liable on summary conviction to a fine not exceeding level 3 on the standard scale.

Uniforms and badges

6   For the purposes of paragraphs 4 and 5, a detainee custody officer is not to be regarded as acting in accordance with escort arrangements at any time when he is not readily identifiable as such an officer (whether by means of a uniform or badge which he is wearing or otherwise).

Suspension and revocation of certificates of authorisation

7(1) If it appears to the Secretary of State that a detainee custody officer is not a fit and proper person to perform escort functions or custodial functions, he may revoke that officer's certificate so far as it authorises the performance of those functions.

   (2) If it appears to the escort monitor that a detainee custody officer is not a fit and proper person to perform escort functions, he may –

   (a) refer the matter to the Secretary of State; or

   (b) in such circumstances as may be prescribed, suspend the officer's certificate pending a decision by the Secretary of State as to whether to revoke it.

   (3) If it appears to the contract monitor for the removal centre concerned that a detainee custody officer is not a fit and proper person to perform custodial functions, he may –

   (a) refer the matter to the Secretary of State; or

   (b) in such circumstances as may be prescribed, suspend the officer's certificate pending a decision by the Secretary of State as to whether to revoke it.

Prison officers and prisoner custody officers

8   A reference in this Schedule to a detainee custody officer includes a reference to a prison officer or prisoner custody officer exercising custodial functions.

Custodial functions and discipline etc at removal centres

155(1) Custodial functions may be discharged at a removal centre only by –

  (a) a detainee custody officer authorised, in accordance with section 154(1), to perform such functions; or

  (b) a prison officer, or a certified prisoner custody officer, exercising functions in relation to the removal centre –

    (i) in accordance with arrangements made under section 154(5); or

    (ii) as a result of a contract entered into under section 150(1)(b).

(2) Schedule 12 makes provision with respect to discipline and other matters at removal centres and short-term holding facilities.

Short-term holding facilities

157(1) The Secretary of State may by regulations extend any provision made by or under this Part in relation to removal centres (other than one mentioned in subsection (2)) to short-term holding facilities.

(2) Subsection (1) does not apply to section 150.

(3) The Secretary of State may make rules for the regulation and management of short-term holding facilities.

Under s 147 of the 1999 Act, '"short-term holding facility" means a place used solely for the detention of detained persons for a period of not more than seven days or for such other period as may be prescribed'. The amended s 147, *inter alia*, also states that '"removal centre" means a place which is used solely for the detention of detained persons but which is not a short-term holding facility, a prison or part of a prison'.

As will be observed above, paras 4 and 5 of Sched 11 to the 1999 Act create the offences of assault, resisting or wilfully obstructing detainee custody officers, and attach the same maximum penalties as those applicable to prisoner custody officers and custody officers (as well as magistrates' court security officers). The question of enforcement regarding these offences emerges yet again. The same anomalies mentioned above in relation to these also seem to apply to detainee custody officers.[1] The exception is where prison officers are used instead of officers from the private sector. Section 8 of the Prison Act 1952, as mentioned earlier, confers all the powers of a constable on prison officers in the course of their duty, and this is reinforced by s 154(6) of the 1999 Act, but the private sector officers are excluded from the ambit of this provision. The problem of arrest powers does not arise where detainee custody officers are assaulted by a person in possession of a real or imitation firearm. Under para 5C of Sched 1 to the Firearms Act 1968, this is an offence punishable by a maximum of life imprisonment. This clearly falls within the scope of being an arrestable offence under s 24 and Sched 1A of PACE. Under certain circumstances, such actions could possibly fall within the scope of a serious arrestable offence. As mentioned above, this offence is also applicable with regard to the protection of prisoner custody officers and secure training centre custody officers.

---

1   For a full commentary on these provisions, refer to Jason-Lloyd, L, 'Part VIII of the Immigration and Asylum Act 1999 – further contracting-out of custodial services' (2000) 164(24) Justice of the Peace, pp 456–60.

All immigration removal centres, whether directly or privately-managed, are under the general control of a manager, who is subject to removal centre rules. In the case of privately-managed centres, the manager is overseen by a Crown servant known as a contract monitor. This broadly reflects the management structure of other privately-managed custodial institutions, mentioned above, regarding the prisons and the secure training centres. However, whilst immigration removal centres may be directly-managed or privately-run, it is possible for a centre to be partly contracted out. A contract monitor is under a duty to investigate complaints against detainee custody officers (or any other class of person performing custodial duties) and may have the responsibility of reviewing more than one immigration removal centre.

In the event of a manager losing control of all or part of a privately-managed removal centre, or if there is a likelihood of this occurring, the Secretary of State may exercise the power to appoint a Crown servant known as a controller. Under s 151 of the 1999 Act, the controller will then temporarily replace the manager and the contract monitor until order has been restored. This also reflects similar provisions applicable to the privately-managed prisons and secure training centres. The managers of the privately-run centres, unlike their counterparts within those centres that are directly-managed, do not have the power to exercise disciplinary measures against detainees. The only exception is in an emergency, where it is necessary to exercise certain segregation and restraint measures:

Management of removal centres

148(1) A manager must be appointed for every removal centre.

(2) In the case of a contracted out removal centre, the person appointed as manager must be a detainee custody officer whose appointment is approved by the Secretary of State.

(3) The manager of a removal centre is to have such functions as are conferred on him by removal centre rules.

(4) The manager of a contracted out removal centre may not –

(a) enquire into a disciplinary charge laid against a detained person;

(b) conduct the hearing of such a charge; or

(c) make, remit or mitigate an award in respect of such a charge.

(5) The manager of a contracted out removal centre may not, except in cases of urgency, order –

(a) the removal of a detained person from association with other detained persons;

(b) the temporary confinement of a detained person in special accommodation; or

(c) the application to a detained person of any other special control or restraint (other than handcuffs).

Contracting out of certain removal centres

149(1) The Secretary of State may enter into a contract with another person for the provision or running (or the provision and running) by him, or (if the contract so provides) for the running by sub-contractors of his, of any removal centre or part of a removal centre.

(2) While a removal centre contract for the running of a removal centre or part of a removal centre is in force –

(a) the removal centre or part is to be run subject to and in accordance with the provisions of or made under this Part; and

(b) in the case of a part, that part and the remaining part are to be treated for the purposes of those provisions as if they were separate removal centres.

(3) If the Secretary of State grants a lease or tenancy of land for the purposes of a removal centre contract, none of the following enactments applies to the lease or tenancy –

(a) Part II of the Landlord and Tenant Act 1954 (security of tenure);

(b) section 146 of the Law of Property Act 1925 (restrictions on and relief against forfeiture);

(c) section 19(1), (2) and (3) of the Landlord and Tenant Act 1927 and the Landlord and Tenant Act 1988 (covenant not to assign etc);

(d) the Agricultural Holdings Act 1986;

(e) sections 4 to 7 of the Law Reform (Miscellaneous Provisions) (Scotland) Act 1985 (irritancy clauses);

(f) the Agricultural Holdings (Scotland) Act 1991;

(g) section 14 of the Conveyancing Act 1881;

(h) the Conveyancing and Law of Property Act 1892;

(i) the Business Tenancies (Northern Ireland) Order 1996.

(4) The Secretary of State must appoint a contract monitor for every contracted out removal centre.

(5) A person may be appointed as the contract monitor for more than one removal centre.

(6) The contract monitor is to have –

(a) such functions as may be conferred on him by removal centre rules;

(b) the status of a Crown servant.

(7) The contract monitor must –

(a) keep under review, and report to the Secretary of State on, the running of a removal centre for which he is appointed; and

(b) investigate, and report to the Secretary of State on, any allegations made against any person performing custodial duties at that centre.

(8) The contractor, and any sub-contractor of his, must do all that he reasonably can (whether by giving directions to the officers of the removal centre or otherwise) to facilitate the exercise by the contractor monitor of his functions.

(9) 'Lease or tenancy' includes an underlease, sublease or subtenancy.

(10) In relation to a removal centre contract entered into by the Secretary of State before the commencement of this section, this section is to be treated as having been in force at that time.

Intervention by Secretary of State

151(1) The Secretary of State may exercise the powers conferred by this section if it appears to him that –

(a) the manager of a contracted out removal centre has lost, or is likely to lose, effective control of the centre or any part of it; or

    (b) it is necessary to do so in the interests of preserving the safety of any person, or of preventing serious damage to any property.

(2) The Secretary of State may appoint a person (to be known as the Controller, to act as manager of the removal centre for the period –

    (a) beginning with the time specified in the appointment; and

    (b) ending with the time specified in the notice of termination under subsection (5).

(3) During that period –

    (a) all the functions which would otherwise be exercisable by the manager or the contract monitor are to be exercisable by the Controller;

    (b) the contractor and any sub-contractor of his must do all that he reasonably can to facilitate the exercise by the Controller of his functions; and

    (c) the staff of the removal centre must comply with any directions given by the Controller in the exercise of his functions.

(4) The Controller is to have the status of a Crown servant.

(5) If the Secretary of State is satisfied that a Controller is no longer needed for a particular removal centre, he must (by giving notice to the Controller) terminate his appointment at a time specified in the notice.

(6) As soon as practicable after making an appointment under this section, the Secretary of State must give notice of the appointment to those entitled to notice.

(7) As soon as practicable after terminating an appointment under this section, the Secretary of State must give a copy of the notice of termination to those entitled to notice.

(8) Those entitled to notice are the contractor, the manager, the contract monitor and the Controller.

Matters such as the safety, care, discipline and control of immigration detainees fall within more specific provisions regarding the regulation and management of the immigration removal centres. These are to be found under 'removal centre rules', which are made by the Secretary of State under s 153 of the 1999 Act (see also Sched 12). Section 152, however, makes provision for the inspection of all immigration removal centres by visiting committees. Each centre has its own committee whose duties include hearing complaints by the detainees. Although there are no express provisions to appoint visiting committees to short-term holding centres, s 157 of the 1999 Act enables the Secretary of State to do this if he sees fit. This is because nearly all the regulations regarding immigration removal centres can also be applied to places providing short-term holding facilities. As mentioned above, the definition of the latter is to be found under s 147 which states that '"short-term holding facility" means a place used solely for the detention of detained persons for a period of not more than seven days or for such other period as may be prescribed':

Visiting committees and inspections

152(1) The Secretary of State must appoint a committee (to be known as the Visiting Committee) for each removal centre.

    (2) The functions of the Visiting Committee for a removal centre are to be such as may be prescribed by the removal centre rules.

(3) Those rules must include provision –

    (a) as to the making of visits to the centre by members of the Visiting Committee;

    (b) for the hearing of complaints made by persons detained in the centre;

    (c) requiring the making of reports by the Visiting Committee to the Secretary of State.

(4) Every member of the Visiting Committee for a removal centre may at any time enter the centre and have free access to every part of it and to every person detained there.

(5) In section 5A of the Prison Act 1952 (which deals with the appointment and functions of Her Majesty's Chief Inspector of Prisons), after subsection (5), insert –

(5A) Subsections (2) to (5) apply to removal centres (as defined by section 147 of the Immigration and Asylum Act 1999 and including any in Scotland) and persons detained in such removal centres as they apply to prisons and prisoners.

The escort arrangements regarding immigration detainees are contained under s 156 and Sched 13 to the 1999 Act. These arrangements may be contracted out and performed by trained and certificated detainee custody officers or prisoner custody officers. Paragraph 3 of Sched 11 to the 1999 Act provides that detainee custody officers, authorised only to perform escort duties, may be used for custodial duties at the short-term holding facilities. The powers and duties of the operatives engaged in escort duties are almost identical to those described above, regarding prisoner custody officers and custody officers. Paragraph 1 of Sched 13 to the 1999 Act makes very similar provisions to those under the Criminal Justice Act 1991 and the Criminal Justice and Public Order Act 1994, in respect of an escort monitor. There is, however, one difference: that is, the monitor under the 1999 Act does not have a team of lay observers to inspect the conditions under which the detainees are held. According to the wording of these provisions, this has to be done personally by the monitor:

Arrangements for the provision of escorts and custody

156(1) The Secretary of State may make arrangements for –

    (a) the delivery of detained persons to premises in which they may lawfully be detained;

    (b) the delivery of persons from any such premises for the purposes of their removal from the United Kingdom in accordance with directions given under the 1971 Act or this Act;

    (c) the custody of detained persons who are temporarily outside such premises;

    (d) the custody of detained persons held on the premises of any court.

(2) Escort arrangements may provide for functions under the arrangements to be performed, in such cases as may be determined by or under the arrangements, by detainee custody officers.

(3) 'Court' includes –

    (a) adjudicators;

    (b) the Immigration Appeal Tribunal;

    (c) the Commission.

(4) Escort arrangements may include entering into contracts with other persons for the provision by them of –

(a) detainee custody officers; or

(b) prisoner custody officers who are certified under section 89 of the Criminal Justice Act 1991, or section 114 or 122 of the Criminal Justice and Public Order Act 1994, to perform escort functions.

(5) Schedule 13 makes further provision about escort arrangements.

(6) A person responsible for performing a function of a kind mentioned in subsection (1), in accordance with a transfer direction, complies with the direction if he does all that he reasonably can to secure that the function is performed by a person acting in accordance with escort arrangements.

(7) 'Transfer direction' means a transfer direction given under –

(a) section 48 of the Mental Health Act 1983 or section 71 of the Mental Health (Scotland) Act 1984 (removal to hospital of, among others, persons detained under the 1971 Act); or

(b) in Northern Ireland, article 54 of the Mental Health (Northern Ireland) Order 1986 (provision corresponding to section 48 of the 1983 Act).

SCHEDULE 13
ESCORT ARRANGEMENTS

Monitoring of escort arrangements

1(1) Escort arrangements must include provision for the appointment of a Crown servant as escort monitor.

(2) The escort monitor must –

(a) keep the escort arrangements under review and report on them to the Secretary of State as required in accordance with the arrangements;

(b) from time to time inspect the conditions in which detained persons are transported or held in accordance with the escort arrangements;

(c) make recommendations to the Secretary of State, with a view to improving those conditions, whenever he considers it appropriate to do so;

(d) investigate, and report to the Secretary of State on, any allegation made against a detainee custody officer or prisoner custody officer in respect of any act done, or failure to act, when carrying out functions under the arrangements.

(3) Paragraph (d) of sub-paragraph (2) does not apply in relation to –

(a) detainee custody officers employed as part of the Secretary of State's staff; or

(b) an act or omission of a prisoner custody officer so far as it falls to be investigated by a prisoner escort monitor under section 81 of the Criminal Justice Act 1991 or under section 103 or 119 of the Criminal Justice and Public Order Act 1994.

Powers and duties of detainee custody officers

2(1) A detainee custody officer acting in accordance with escort arrangements has power –

(a) to search (in accordance with rules made by the Secretary of State) any detained person for whose delivery or custody the officer is responsible in accordance with the arrangements; and

(b) to search any other person who is in, or is seeking to enter, any place where any such detained person is or is to be held, and any article in the possession of such a person.

(2) The power conferred by sub-paragraph (1)(b) does not authorise requiring a person to remove any of his clothing other than an outer coat, jacket or glove.

(3) As respects a detained person for whose delivery or custody he is responsible in accordance with escort arrangements, it is the duty of a detainee custody officer –

(a) to prevent that person's escape from lawful custody;

(b) to prevent, or detect and report on, the commission or attempted commission by him of other unlawful acts;

(c) to ensure good order and discipline on his part; and

(d) to attend to his wellbeing.

(4) The Secretary of State may make rules with respect to the performance by detainee custody officers of their duty under sub-paragraph (3)(d).

(5) The powers conferred by sub-paragraph (1), and the powers arising by virtue of sub-paragraph (3), include power to use reasonable force where necessary.

Breaches of discipline

3(1) Sub-paragraph (2) applies if a detained person for whose delivery or custody a person ('A') has been responsible in accordance with escort arrangements is delivered to a removal centre.

(2) The detained person is to be treated, for the purposes of such removal centre rules as relate to disciplinary offences, as if he had been in the custody of the director of the removal centre at all times while A was so responsible.

(3) Sub-paragraph (4) applies if a detained person for whose delivery or custody a person ('B') has been responsible in accordance with escort arrangements is delivered to a prison.

(4) The detained person is to be treated, for the purposes of such prison rules as relate to disciplinary offences, as if he had been in the custody of the governor or controller of the prison at all times while B was so responsible.

(5) 'Director' means –

(a) in the case of a contracted out removal centre, the person appointed by the Secretary of State in relation to the centre under section 149 or such other person as the Secretary of State may appoint for the purposes of this paragraph;

(b) in the case of any other removal centre, the manager of the removal centre.

(6) This paragraph does not authorise the punishment of a detained person under removal centre rules or prison rules in respect of any act or omission of his for which he has already been punished by a court.

(7) 'Prison rules' means –

(a) rules made under section 47 of the Prison Act 1952;

(b) rules made under section 19 of the Prisons (Scotland) Act 1989;

(c) rules made under section 13 of the Prison Act (Northern Ireland) 1953.

All personnel working for the immigration removal centres or the escort service, whether or not they are detainee custody officers or prisoner custody officers, commit an offence by making unauthorised disclosure about any detainee. This also applies to former employees. This is modelled on the provisions with regard to prisoner custody officers and ancillary staff, under the Criminal Justice Act 1991, and custody officers and ancillary staff, under the Criminal Justice and Public Order Act 1994. The same criminal sanctions apply on conviction, as stated under s 158 of the 1999 Act as follows:

Wrongful disclosure of information

158(1) A person who is or has been employed (whether as a detainee custody officer, prisoner custody officer or otherwise) –

(a) in accordance with escort arrangements,

(b) at a contracted out removal centre, or

(c) to perform contracted out functions at a directly managed removal centre,

is guilty of an offence if he discloses, otherwise than in the course of his duty or as authorised by the Secretary of State, any information which he acquired in the course of his employment and which relates to a particular detained person.

(2) A person guilty of such an offence is liable –

(a) on conviction on indictment, to imprisonment for a term not exceeding two years or to a fine or to both;

(b) on summary conviction, to imprisonment for a term not exceeding six months or to a fine not exceeding the statutory maximum or to both.

(3) 'Contracted out functions' means functions which, as the result of a contract entered into under section 150, fall to be performed by detainee custody officers or certified prisoner custody officers.

At the time of writing, there are nine immigration removal centres in this country. Three are managed by the prison service on behalf of the immigration service and six are privately-managed.

It is important not to confuse the immigration removal centres (or temporary holding facilities) with accommodation centres instituted under Pt 2 of the Nationality, Immigration and Asylum Act 2002. This Part of the Act enables the Home Secretary to provide premises for use as accommodation centres for destitute or near-destitute asylum seekers and their dependants. These centres will provide a range of essential services such as food and healthcare, as well as financial assistance. The provision of these premises may be made through the private sector or by local authorities. However, they are not custodial institutions and should therefore be distinguished from immigration removal centres and the temporary holding facilities.

CHANGES TO THE POWERS OF DETAINEE CUSTODY OFFICERS UNDER THE NATIONALITY, IMMIGRATION AND ASYLUM ACT 2002

The Nationality, Immigration and Asylum Act 2002 has made a number of significant changes to the Immigration and Asylum Act 1999 regarding the detention of certain immigrants. First, as already mentioned at the beginning of this chapter, s 66 of the 2002 Act changed the name of the previously-entitled immigration detention centres to immigration removal centres. Secondly, s 64 extends para 17 of Sched 2 to the Immigration Act 1971 and gives an additional power to detainee custody officers whilst on escort duties. This will enable them to enter premises, using reasonable force if necessary, in order to search a detained person before escorting him or her to the relevant place of detention. The initial detention of that person will be made by a police officer or immigration officer as a result of executing a warrant under para 17(2) of Sched 2 to the Immigration Act 1971. Thirdly, s 153 of the 2002 Act inserts a new s 28CA into the 1971 Act which provides police and immigration officers with the power to search business premises and also to arrest immigration offenders who are on those premises. Where police or immigration officers detain such persons on those premises, a detainee custody officer may then enter, using reasonable force if necessary, in order to carry out a search in pursuance of his or her escort duties.

CHAPTER 6

CHANNEL TUNNEL SECURITY

The overall security arrangements regarding the Channel Tunnel are contained under The Channel Tunnel (Security) Order 1994.[1] This Order, *inter alia*, states the provisions governing civilian search powers arising from the Secretary of State for Transport, giving written directives to the concessionaires of the Channel Tunnel, and others, to conduct searches. For the purposes of this chapter, the main provisions under this Order are Arts 13, 14, 15, 31 and 32. Article 13 is subheaded 'Power to impose restrictions in relation to Channel Tunnel trains', and sub-s (1) states that:

> For purposes to which this Part of this Order applies, the Secretary of State may give a direction in writing to the Concessionaires or to the owner, operator or train manager of any Channel Tunnel train requiring that person –
>
> (a) not to cause or permit persons or property to go or be taken on board any Channel Tunnel train to which the direction relates, or to come or be brought into proximity to any such Channel Tunnel train, unless such searches of those persons or that property as are specified in the direction have been carried out by persons of a description specified in the direction or by constables, or
>
> (b) not to cause or permit any such Channel Tunnel train to be put into service or moved unless such searches of the train as are specified in the direction have been carried out by persons of a description so specified or by constables.

The empowerment of certain civilians, as well as the police, to conduct searches in fulfilment of the above requirements is clearly indicated by the words 'persons of a description specified in the direction' and 'persons of a description so specified'. This is replicated in the relevant Articles, which will be mentioned below. The power to use reasonable force in order to conduct a search under these provisions is absent here. It is submitted that this may be due to these searches being a condition of entry onto a train or entry to the close proximity of one, as well as being a condition of the train being put into service or moved. However, sub-s (6) states that:

> Subject to the following provisions of this Part of this Order, any direction given under this article to any person not to cause or permit anything to be done shall be construed as requiring him to take all such steps as in any particular circumstances are practicable and necessary to prevent that thing from being done.

Does the taking of such steps include the use of reasonable force? In any event, Art 32 makes the following provisions regarding persons who obstruct or impersonate those acting under these and other powers:

> (1) A person who –
>
> (a) intentionally obstructs an authorised person acting in the exercise of a power conferred on him by or under this Part of this Order; or

---

(b) falsely pretends to be an authorised person,

commits an offence.

(2) A person guilty of an offence under paragraph (1)(a) above is liable –

    (a) on summary conviction, to a fine not exceeding the statutory maximum;[2]

    (b) on conviction on indictment, to a fine or to imprisonment for a term not exceeding two years or to both.

(3) A person guilty of an offence under paragraph (1)(b) above is liable on summary conviction to a fine not exceeding level 5[3] on the standard scale.[4]

Article 14 is subheaded 'Power to require the Concessionaires to promote searches in the tunnel system', and sub-s (1) makes the following provisions:

> For the purposes to which this Part of this Order applies, the Secretary of State may give a direction in writing to the Concessionaires requiring them to use their best endeavours to secure that such searches to which this Article applies as are specified in the direction are carried out by persons of a description specified in the direction or by constables.

Sub-section (2) describes the searches applicable to Art 14, namely, searches of the Tunnel or any part of it, as well as persons and property, and any Channel Tunnel train which may be in the Tunnel at the time. Sub-section (3) states that when a direction is in force, a 'person of a description specified in the direction', or a constable, may search the foregoing without warrant if that person has reasonable grounds to suspect that any of the following articles are in, or may be brought into, any part of the tunnel system: firearms or explosives (real or imitation), ammunition or offensive weapons. In order to achieve this purpose, such persons may enter any building or works in the Tunnel system, using force if necessary. They may stop, board and detain any Channel Tunnel train and inspect it, and may stop and detain any vehicle, goods, property or person for as long as necessary. Under Art 18(2), reasonable force may be used in the exercise of these search powers. Anyone who intentionally obstructs a person exercising these powers commits an offence, which is triable either way and punishable by a fine not exceeding £5,000 if tried summarily, or a maximum of two years' imprisonment and/or an unlimited fine if tried on indictment.

Article 15 broadly replicates the provisions of Art 14, except that it applies to directions by the Secretary of State to persons other than the concessionaires. This includes those who have official access to restricted areas within the Tunnel and those who carry on operations in the Tunnel system, or have responsibility for the management of any property used in connection with the operation of Tunnel system. This also includes those responsible for the management of

---

2   The current maximum is £5,000.

3   The maximum under level 5 is also £5,000.

4   The explanatory note attached to the Channel Tunnel (Security) Order 1994 states that these offences apply to 'a person authorised in writing by the Secretary of State for the purposes of Pt III of the Order when acting in the exercise of his powers'. It also creates an offence of falsely pretending to be such a person. It is submitted that this may also extend to those acting under the instructions of such a person and therefore includes those at ground level who conduct such searches. It seems logical that since obstruction and impersonation can occur at all levels, Art 32 may have been intended to be a catch-all provision.

Channel Tunnel trains. The search powers exercisable under Art 15 are also available to certain civilians, as well as the police, and Art 18(2) provides that reasonable force may be used in the exercise of these powers. Also, the same penalties on conviction for obstructing such searches apply to this Article as they do under Art 14.

Article 31 concerns the unauthorised presence of persons in a clearly marked restricted zone, and makes it an offence to enter such a place without permission or to remain there, having been asked to leave by a constable or by 'the person in control of the restricted zone or a person acting on his behalf'. Reasonable force may be used by the police, or the person in control of the restricted zone, to remove a person who refuses to leave. Note that the person in control of a restricted zone or his representative will be a civilian. The provisions of Art 32, mentioned above, should also be noted with regard to the offences of obstructing and impersonating authorised persons acting under the powers conferred by Pt III of this Order.

It will be apparent that no specific powers of arrest are attached to the offences of intentionally obstructing or impersonating a civilian authorised to conduct searches or exercise other special powers within and around the Channel Tunnel. Therefore, how are those who commit such offences to be prosecuted? None of them are arrestable under s 24 of PACE 1984, and only the police can use the general arrest conditions under s 25 of the 1984 Act, in the event of a refusal to provide a name and address for the service of a summons or where the particulars given are unsatisfactory.

The above observation again reflects the apparent omissions in the special powers available to all those classes of private security personnel discussed in previous chapters. It could be argued that, in the absence of specific arrest powers in this context, the police could be called to deal with the suspect. However, civilian security personnel have been created largely to replace the police, who may not be readily available to deal with such an incident. It will be interesting to see how this issue is dealt with, should such matters be brought before the courts. Perhaps the regulation of the private security industry may, *inter alia*, motivate the rationalisation of what appears to be a rather incomplete package of special powers available to private security operatives performing public protection duties.[5] In the event of offences being disclosed in the course of their duties, excluding those relating to obstructing, resisting, assaulting or impersonating them, the civilians given the above special powers would have to rely on those available to ordinary citizens. These will include s 3(1) of the Criminal Law Act 1967, s 24 of PACE and the common law power to deal with or prevent a breach of the peace. As discussed in previous chapters, there are still limitations regarding the use of these powers.

5   For coverage of the regulation of the private security industry, see Chapter 11.

CHAPTER 7

CIVILIAN ENFORCEMENT OFFICERS UNDER THE ACCESS TO JUSTICE ACT 1999

Under Pt V of the Access to Justice Act 1999, civilian enforcement officers may be employed by magistrates' courts committees to execute arrest warrants and warrants of commitment, detention or distress issued by justices of the peace. This task was often performed by the police, although for some years prior to the 1999 Act, civilian enforcement officers had been used to execute warrants, albeit in a more limited range of circumstances, such as unpaid fines. The 1999 Act has significantly increased the scope of warrants that they may execute, as well as enabling the contracting out of such tasks to approved enforcement agencies.

In s 92 of the 1999 Act, which inserts a new s 125A into the Magistrates' Courts Act 1980, the range of warrants that may be executed by civilian enforcement officers include the following:

- warrants of distress (seizure of a fine defaulter's money or goods in lieu of the outstanding amount);
- warrants of commitment (committing a defaulter to prison);
- warrants for overnight detention in a police station;
- warrants of arrest to bring a defaulter before the court;
- warrants under the Child Support Act 1991;
- warrants of arrest and commitment issued under regs 47(3)(a) and 48(5)(b) of the Council Tax (Administration and Enforcement) Regulations 1989;
- warrants of arrest and commitment issued under regs 16(3)(a) and 17(5)(b) of the Non-Domestic Rating (Collection etc) Regulations 1989;
- warrants of arrest and commitment issued under regs 41(1) and 42(5)(b) of the Community Charges Regulations 1989; and
- confiscation orders.

Also included are arrest warrants to secure the attendance in court of persons in breach of community sentences, as well as for breaches of conditions of other sentences.

The full text of the new s 125A of the Magistrates' Courts Act 1980, as inserted by s 92 of the Access to Justice Act 1999, is as follows:

Civilian enforcement officers

92   In the Magistrates' Courts Act 1980, after section 125 insert –

'**Civilian enforcement officers**

125A(1)A warrant to which this subsection applies may be executed anywhere in England and Wales by a civilian enforcement officer.

(2) In this section "civilian enforcement officer", in relation to a warrant, means a person who –

(a) is employed by an authority of a prescribed class which performs functions in relation to any area specified in the warrant; and

(b) is authorised in the prescribed manner to execute warrants.

(3) The warrants to which subsection (1) above applies are any warrant of arrest, commitment, detention or distress issued by a justice of the peace –

(a) under any provision specified for the purposes of this subsection by an order made by the Lord Chancellor and the Secretary of State, acting jointly; or

(b) for the enforcement of a court order of any description so specified.

(4) Where a warrant has been executed by a civilian enforcement officer, a written statement indicating –

(a) the name of the officer;

(b) the authority by which he is employed; and

(c) that he is authorised in the prescribed manner to execute warrants,

shall, on the demand of the person arrested, committed or detained or against whom distress is levied, be shown to him as soon as practicable.

(5) The power to make orders conferred by subsection (3) above shall be exercisable by statutory instrument which shall be subject to annulment in pursuance of a resolution of either House of Parliament.'

As mentioned above, the 1999 Act has enabled the execution of routine arrest warrants to be contracted out to approved enforcement agencies. This is provided under s 93, which amends the Justices of the Peace Act 1997 and the Magistrates' Courts Act 1980, as follows:

Approved enforcement agencies

93(1) In the Justices of the Peace Act 1997, after section 31 insert –

'Execution of warrants

31A(1) A magistrates' courts committee may approve persons or bodies for the purpose of executing warrants pursuant to section 125B of the Magistrates' Courts Act 1980.

(2) The Lord Chancellor may by statutory instrument make regulations as to –

(a) conditions which must be satisfied by a person or body in order to be approved under subsection (1) above; and

(b) the procedure by which a person or body may be so approved.

(3) A statutory instrument containing (whether alone or with other provisions) regulations made by virtue of subsection (2) above shall be subject to annulment in pursuance of a resolution of either House of Parliament.

(4) A magistrates' courts committee shall maintain a register –

(a) containing the names of all persons and bodies approved by the committee under subsection (1) above; or

(b) stating that no person or body has been so approved.

(5) Copies of the register kept by a committee under subsection (4) above shall be available for inspection by members of the public in every petty sessional court-house in the committee's area during the hours that the court-house is open to the public.

(6) A decision by a magistrates' courts committee to revoke the approval of a person or body under subsection (1) above does not have effect to revoke the approval until the committee have informed the person or body in writing of the decision.'

93(2) In the Magistrates' Courts Act 1980, after section 125A (inserted by section 92 above) insert –

'Execution by approved enforcement agency

125B(1) A warrant to which section 125A(1) above applies may also be executed anywhere in England and Wales –

    (a) by an individual who is an approved enforcement agency;

    (b) by a director of a company which is an approved enforcement agency;

    (c) by a partner in a partnership which is an approved enforcement agency; or

    (d) by an employee of an approved enforcement agency who is authorised in writing by the agency to execute warrants.

  (2) In this section "approved enforcement agency", in relation to a warrant, means a person or body approved under section 31A of the Justices of the Peace Act 1997 by the magistrates' courts committee for the petty sessions area of the justice (or any of the justices) who issued the warrant.

  (3) Failure by a magistrates' courts committee to comply with any provision of, or made under, section 31A(2) to (5) of the Justices of the Peace Act 1997 does not of itself render unlawful the execution of a warrant.

  (4) Where a warrant has been executed by a person mentioned in subsection (1) above, a written statement indicating the matters specified in subsection (5) below shall, on the demand of the person arrested, committed or detained or against whom distress is levied, be shown to him as soon as practicable.

  (5) The matters referred to in subsection (4) above are –

    (a) the name of the person by whom the warrant was executed;

    (b) if he is a director of, or partner in, an approved enforcement agency, the fact that he is a director of, or a partner in, that agency;

    (c) if he is an employee of an approved enforcement agency, the fact that he is an employee authorised in writing by that agency to execute warrants; and

    (d) the fact that his name, or (where paragraph (b) or (c) above applies) that of the agency indicated, is contained in the register maintained under section 31A(4) of the Justices of the Peace Act 1997 by the magistrates' courts committee concerned.'

No express provisions are made under the 1999 Act for the use of reasonable force, where necessary, in the execution of warrants by civilian enforcement officers. In the absence of specific powers, it is possible they may rely on s 3(1) of the Criminal Law Act 1967 when executing warrants of arrest. Also, there are no specific offences of assaulting, resisting or obstructing these civilian enforcement officers, although an offence under s 38 of the Offences Against the Person Act 1861 may apply. This is the offence of assault with intent to resist arrest, which is triable either way and carries a maximum of two years' imprisonment when tried on indictment. Realistically, it would appear that such officers may adopt a non-confrontational stance in situations where there is significant resistance to the execution of a warrant.

The rules mentioned above under s 93 of the 1999 Act, regarding approved enforcement agencies, are contained under SI 2000/3279. Interestingly, two magistrates' court committees have recently given their warrant enforcement back to the police under contract. For future reference, the current Courts Bill 'includes provisions to create the role of fines officers and to introduce a range of new sanctions to improve the effectiveness of fine enforcement'. These may include a 'clamping order' which involves wheelclamping the vehicles of fine defaulters which, in turn, may be sold later if the fine is not settled.

PART II:
DESIGNATED AND
ACCREDITED CIVILIANS
UNDER THE POLICE
REFORM ACT 2002:
THE 'EXTENDED
POLICE FAMILY'

CHAPTER 8

DESIGNATED CIVILIANS: COMMUNITY SUPPORT OFFICERS, INVESTIGATING OFFICERS, DETENTION OFFICERS AND ESCORT OFFICERS

This book would not be complete without coverage of another stratum of law enforcement and crime prevention that has been created very recently. Part 4, Chapter 1 of the Police Reform Act 2002, together with Scheds 4 and 5, contains a range of provisions which will enable the performance of specific policing duties by certain civilians. The complete text of Pt 4, Chapter 1 and Scheds 4 and 5 of the Police Reform Act 2002 are reproduced in Appendix 4. The designated civilians referred to may also be given special powers in the performance of these tasks, although far greater than those discussed in Part I of this book. This new development has been included here because it also falls under the heading of quasi-policing. In fact, these latest measures, among other things, may constitute the biggest single move towards bringing the private security industry directly into public policing. Whether this will prove to be an effective and harmonious relationship remains to be seen. In the meantime, there could be a substantial period of compromise and adjustment before this stage is reached.

During the time that this book was being written, about 65% of all police forces in England and Wales were beginning to participate in a scheme involving the use of community support officers (CSOs). These constitute just one of several classes of designated civilians under the 2002 Act. At least one of these participating police forces is already using CSOs with varying powers and, in some cases, no special powers at all. The police forces that are part of this project have been listed at the end of the section dealing with CSOs (see p 57). This scheme, at least in principle, may constitute an important step forward in creating an 'extended police family' and, subsequently, providing more uniformed law-enforcers in areas where their presence is needed. It should be noted that whilst the 2002 Act refers to these as 'CSOs', it seems that the police service are referring to them as 'police community support officers'. For the sake of brevity, they will be referred to in accordance with the shorter version, as stated in the Act.

Different classes of designated civilians, who are subject to this scheme overall may be directly employed by police or service authorities; a limited range may be contracted in from security companies; or chief officers of police may exercise their option to adopt a community safety accreditation scheme (see Chapter 9, p 67). This will enable them to accredit certain civilian operatives to exercise specific powers within their police area. It has been stated that these accreditation schemes may even extend to the private sector, with regard to the manned guarding of large shopping centres and other commercial sites such as industrial estates.[1] This could also include neighbourhood or community

---

1   See *Security Voice*, the official magazine of the government-sponsored Joint Security Industry Council, Summer 2002, p 23. This contains an interesting speech by the chairman of the Security Industry Authority.

warden schemes, although the conferring of special powers may not always be done automatically, if at all. Certain operatives working in community safety schemes have stated that they do not want special powers, as this could undermine their standing locally. In other instances, however, the need for special powers is considered imperative.

It is intended that designated CSOs should avoid being too confrontational in the exercise of their duties when dealing with the public. Whilst they have been given special powers beyond those normally held by non-police officers, these powers have certain limitations placed upon them that are designed to tacitly define the limits of their involvement in certain incidents. However, in front-line duties, it is often the situation a person is confronted with that determines what they must do, rather than the powers they may have.

It is important to note that, whatever powers may be conferred upon directly employed designated civilians, s 38(7)(b) of the Police Reform Act states that the relevant chief officer of police (or a Director General) may impose restrictions and conditions on those powers. Section 39(7)(b) makes the same provision applicable to police forces using contracted out civilians, namely, detention officers and escort officers.

DIRECTLY EMPLOYED CIVILIANS

Section 38(1) of the 2002 Act enables chief officers of police in England and Wales to designate any person employed by his police authority to perform one or more duties listed under sub-s (2), which are as follows:

(a) a community support officer;

(b) an investigating officer;

(c) a detention officer;

(d) an escort officer.

In other words, the above civilians will be directly employed by the police service, but largely within the police area where they serve (the exception being officers on certain escort duties), and will fall under the direction and control of the relevant chief officer of police. Section 38(3) provides that the Director General of the National Crime Squad (NCS) or the Director General of the National Criminal Intelligence Service (NCIS) may designate persons to become investigating officers in England and Wales. In this instance, they will be employees of the Service Authority of either body and will be under the direction and control of the relevant Director General. Sub-section (4) states that a person must not be designated to perform any of these special duties unless the relevant chief officer of police or the Director General is satisfied that the appointee is both suitable and capable of performing such duties. This includes receiving the appropriate training.

Although a range of special powers are available under the 2002 Act, it is at the discretion of the chief officer of police (or the Director General) as to which powers these officers are allowed to exercise. In other words, all or some of these powers may be conferred on them. This was the cause of significant concern when the Police Reform Bill was debated in Parliament. The main concern was that designated civilians could have varying powers, depending on which areas they were serving. A more consistent or uniform approach was suggested, but this was resisted on the grounds that these powers should be tailored to local needs.

Section 38 goes on to state certain powers, and the constraints on those powers, which are common to all types of designated civilians under the 2002 Act. In sub-s (7), it is provided that they shall be subject to the imposition of any restrictions and conditions regarding their designation and that they must not engage in conduct outside the scope of their employment. This includes not exceeding the bounds of any powers conferred upon them, nor placing themselves on duty when not working, as police officers may do in appropriate circumstances. Also, under sub-s (8), when a civilian exercises any designated power, which is the same as a power which a police officer may exercise, and the use of reasonable force, where necessary, is part of that power, that designated civilian may use reasonable force in the same circumstances. Finally, under sub-s (9), where a power to use force in order to enter premises is part of a designated civilian's duties, there are two points that should be noted. First, it must only be executed in the company and under the supervision of a police officer. Secondly, forcible entry may be effected, in order to save life or limb or to prevent serious damage to property, by a designated civilian, who does not have to be accompanied by a police officer.

COMMUNITY SUPPORT OFFICERS (SCHEDULE 4, PART 1)

The powers and duties of civilians, who are designated as CSOs, are to be found under Pt 1 of Sched 4 to the 2002 Act. It is stressed that not all the powers under this schedule may necessarily be given to civilians who are designated for this purpose. The choice of all or some of the powers under the following menu will be at the discretion of individual chief officers of police. Also, they may impose restrictions and conditions on any of these powers.

Paragraph 1: powers to issue fixed penalty notices

Under para 1(2) of Sched 4 to the 2002 Act, the fixed penalty offences to which these powers apply are as follows:

(a) The power of a constable in uniform, or an authorised constable, to give a fixed penalty ticket in respect of the following offences:

- being drunk on a highway, other public place or licensed premises (s 12 of the Licensing Act 1872);
- throwing fireworks in a thoroughfare (s 80 of the Explosives Act 1875);
- knowingly giving a false alarm to a fire brigade (s 31 of the Fire Services Act 1947);
- trespassing on a railway (s 55 of the British Transport Commission Act 1949);

- throwing stones, etc, at trains or other things on railways (s 56 of the British Transport Commission Act 1949);

- buying or attempting to buy alcohol for consumption in a bar in licensed premises by a person under 18 (s 169C(3) of the Licensing Act 1964);

- disorderly behaviour while drunk in a public place (s 91 of the Criminal Justice Act 1967);

- wasting police time or giving false report (s 5(2) of the Criminal Law Act 1967);

- using public telecommunications system for sending message known to be false in order to cause annoyance (s 43(1)(b) of the Telecommunications Act 1984);

- consumption of alcohol in a designated public place (s 12 of the Criminal Justice and Police Act 2001);

- behaviour likely to cause harassment, alarm or distress (s 5 of the Public Order Act 1986).[2]

(b) The power of a constable in uniform to give a person a fixed penalty notice for riding a bicycle on a footway.

(c) The power to give a fixed penalty notice in respect of dog fouling.

(d) The power to give a fixed penalty notice in respect of litter.

Under para 2(6)(b)(i) and (ii), there is also a further power that may be exercised by CSOs (provided that they have been authorised to use it under the appropriate designation), which itself can be subject to various modifications. That power includes issuing a fixed penalty notice in respect of an offence which appears to have caused injury, alarm or distress to any other person, or which involves any other person's property being lost or damaged. This potentially includes a wide range of offences, many of which enable a citizen's arrest. These include the more serious offences against the person that are arrestable under s 24 and Sched 1A of PACE, as well as criminal damage, certain public order offences and harassment. The common law power to deal with or prevent a breach of the peace may also be relevant in certain circumstances, and likewise s 3(1) of the Criminal Law Act 1967.

Will CSOs be expected to issue fixed penalty tickets for such offences, in preference to exercising their rights as citizens to make arrests? In view of the non-confrontational stance that is initially expected of all classes of designated (and accredited) civilians, it would appear that the former may prevail, unless the offence is particularly serious. It should be noted that the wording of para 2(6)(b)(i) and (ii) is rather curious, insofar as it appears to apply only to third parties who are injured, alarmed or distressed, or if their property is lost or damaged. The literal reading of these provisions is that a designated (or

---

2   This list is to be found under Pt 1, Chapter 1 of the Criminal Justice and Police Act 2001 (as amended), which also includes the relevant provisions governing such matters as fixed penalty procedures and enforcement. These offences apply to 18 year olds and above. A police officer must be in uniform when issuing such notices in the street, but these notices may be given in a police station whether or not the police officer is in uniform. However, such officers must be authorised to do so. The police are currently piloting this scheme until August 2003. If it proves successful, this may then be extended to CSOs.

accredited) civilian who is the victim of such conduct, cannot act on his own accord because of the words 'any other person'. However, it may not preclude the intervention of another civilian with such powers, who may be in the immediate vicinity of the incident. Also, if a witness was also nearby who was affected by the conduct in question, that person may constitute the required third party, enabling the CSO victim to directly use his powers.

Paragraph 2: power to detain, etc

The issuing of a fixed penalty ticket requires the correct furnishing of a name and address. Where a CSO who is authorised to use this power has reason to believe that another has committed a relevant offence within his police area, then under para 2(2) of Sched 4, the CSO may require that person to give his name and address. If this is refused, or it is suspected that false or inaccurate details have been given, sub-s (3) provides that the CSO may require that person to wait with him for up to 30 minutes for the arrival of a police officer.[3]

This provision was probably the most controversial and widely publicised aspect of the Police Reform Bill during its passage through Parliament. Much of the debate concerning this measure was highly critical, accompanied by some rather confusing arguments on the technical aspects of this provision. For instance, it is not clear as to whether this constitutes an arrest. If it does, then no mention is made of a caution having to be given or any of the other arrest procedures that are incumbent on the police. There is also no power to search a detained person for weapons, and this could place the arresting officer at risk. However, the main focus of criticism in Parliament is the time restriction imposed on this detention by CSOs. It appears that they will simply have to release a person after 30 minutes if the police do not arrive in time, and this was considered wholly unsatisfactory by many critics in both Houses. Since para 4 of Sched 4 states that reasonable force may be used to prevent a person making off whilst detained for failing to provide correct particulars, this 30 minute time limit seems even more puzzling. A power to detain, rather than arrest, already exists under s 21A of the Football Spectators Act 1989, although this only applies to the police. Section 21A provides that a constable in uniform may detain a British citizen for up to four hours in order to ascertain whether that person may or may not be subject to a football banning order. This period of detention may be increased to six hours on the authority of an officer of at least the rank of inspector. These periods of detention are far longer than those that may be conferred upon CSOs, of course. Also, the police have access to other powers if necessary.

A further controversial provision can be found under sub-s (4), where a person liable to be detained under this power may be given the option to accompany the CSO to a police station. It is respectfully submitted that very few persons to whom this applies are likely to accept this option. In any event, it appears that little or no consideration has been given as to the possible distances involved between the locations of these incidents and the nearest police stations;

---

3   Note that when a police officer is faced with a similar situation, he can rely on s 25 of PACE (general arrest conditions).

also, what mode of transport is to be used if the distance is too great? Paragraph 4 also provides that reasonable force may be used by CSOs to prevent a person from making off while en route to a police station, but is this an arrest? Is there a time limit? Under sub-s (5), making off whilst being initially detained or on the way to a police station is an offence punishable by a maximum level 3 fine (£1,000); therefore, it is not an arrestable offence.[4] Many other questions could arise from these issues, which may have to be settled by the courts or by amending the legislation.

Paragraph 3: power to require name and address of persons acting in an anti-social manner

Provided that they have been designated accordingly, CSOs will have the power of a police officer in uniform to exercise powers under s 50 of the Police Reform Act. Paragraph 3(1) of Sched 4 will enable a designated CSO who has reason to believe that a person has been or is acting in an anti-social manner to require that person to provide their name and address. Failure to provide a name and address, or the giving of false particulars, constitutes an offence under sub-s (2), which is punishable by a maximum level 3 fine (£1,000). CSOs may detain a person who commits any of these offences, but only for a maximum of 30 minutes. The option for the person to accompany the CSO to a police station also applies, and it is an offence to make off whilst being detained or accompanied. Paragraph 4 of Sched 4 enables reasonable force to be used to prevent a person from making off under these circumstances.

Paragraph 4: power to use reasonable force to detain a person

The provisions of para 4 regarding the use of reasonable force have been incorporated into the coverage of paras 2 and 3 above.

Paragraph 5: alcohol consumption in designated public places

Designated CSOs will be able to exercise the powers of a constable under s 12 of the Criminal Justice and Police Act 2001, which initially applied only to the police. Section 12 provides that a police officer has the power to require a person not to consume intoxicating liquor in a designated public place, to surrender intoxicating liquor (except where it is in a sealed container) and to dispose of it accordingly. This applies where the police officer reasonably believes that the person is, or has been, consuming drink in a designated public place, or intends to do so. Failure to comply with such a requirement is an arrestable offence and punishable by a fine not exceeding level 2 on the standard scale (currently £500), although the person must be given prior warning that failure to comply with such a requirement is an offence.

---

4   This offence also applies to refusing to provide a name and address or for giving false particulars.

According to para 5 of Sched 4, designated CSOs will have powers under s 12 of the Criminal Justice and Police Act to impose the same requirements as the police and to dispose of the alcohol accordingly. This poses the question as to how the CSOs will be expected to deal with the failure to comply with any of these requirements, which is an arrestable offence. They could make a citizen's arrest, as this offence falls under s 24 and Sched 1A of PACE, and there appears to be no express provision to the contrary. If this is the case, there is no time limit on the arrest, whereas the 30 minute rule applies to several of the other offences mentioned above, which, potentially at least, may sometimes be more serious. If the person concerned is drunk and disorderly, a CSO could make a citizen's arrest under s 91(1) of the Criminal Justice Act 1967, which states that: 'any person who in any public place is guilty, while drunk, of disorderly behaviour may be arrested without warrant by any person ...' The term 'any person' refers to all citizens (see Appendix 3, p 109); therefore, CSOs could exercise this power in appropriate circumstances.

Paragraph 6: confiscation of alcohol

Paragraph 6 of Sched 4 provides that designated CSOs will have the powers of police officers under s 1 of the Confiscation of Alcohol (Young Persons) Act 1997. This power is similar to s 12 of the Criminal Justice and Police Act 2001, except that it applies to the confiscation and subsequent disposal of alcohol from under-18 year olds and those over that age who are nearby. There is also the requirement that the person's name and address be given. Failure to surrender the alcohol or to provide a name and address is an offence punishable by a maximum level 2 fine (£500). A power of arrest is given to the *police* against anyone who commits this offence, although when s 1 of the 1997 Act is applied to CSOs, this has been expressly removed by para 6. How can such an offence be prosecuted in the apparent absence of express enforcement powers? A CSO could possibly use the 'any person' arrest power under s 91(1) of the Criminal Justice Act 1967, as mentioned above, but this would only apply where a person was drunk and disorderly and not merely drinking.

Paragraph 7: confiscation of tobacco, etc

Paragraph 7 of Sched 4 will enable designated CSOs to have the power of a constable in uniform to confiscate tobacco and cigarette papers from under-16 year olds in public places. This power is under s 7(3) of the Children and Young Persons Act 1933, which includes disposing of the items seized. Interestingly, this power is also held by uniformed park keepers. In the case of CSOs, the power to dispose of any such items must be done in a manner as the relevant police authority may direct.

Paragraph 8: entry to save life or limb or prevent serious damage to property

Paragraph 8 of Sched 4 provides that certain designated CSOs will be given the same powers as a constable under s 17 of PACE. This will enable them to enter and search any premises in order to save life or limb or to prevent serious damage to property, whether or not they are accompanied by a police officer. Reasonable force may be used in order to perform this duty, in accordance with s 38(8) of the 2002 Act, which states:

> Where any power exercisable by any person in reliance on his designation under this section is a power which, in the case of its exercise by a constable, includes or is supplemented by a power to use reasonable force, any person exercising that power in reliance on that designation shall have the same entitlement as a constable to use reasonable force.

Paragraph 9: seizure of vehicles used to cause alarm, etc

Under s 59 of the 2002 Act, a new power has been given to the police in order to deal with motor vehicles that are driven carelessly and inconsiderately, or driven off the road, and which cause, or are likely to cause, alarm, distress or annoyance to the public. A constable in uniform who reasonably believes that a motor vehicle is being used in this manner has the power to stop a moving motor vehicle and seize and remove it. The latter may be done by entering premises, except a private dwelling house, and reasonable force may be used to effect any of these powers. However, these may not usually occur unless specific warnings have been given, which are described in sub-ss (4) and (5). Also, none of these powers may be exercised until regulations have been made by the Home Secretary. Failure to stop when ordered to do so by a constable in uniform is an offence punishable by a maximum level 3 fine (£1,000).

Paragraph 9 of Sched 4 enables designated CSOs to exercise all the above powers of a constable, with the exception of a modification to the power to enter premises. In the case of a CSO, this must be done only in the presence of a police officer.

Paragraph 10: abandoned vehicles

Various regulations made under s 99 of the Road Traffic Regulation Act 1984 include the power for the police to remove, or arrange for the removal of, abandoned vehicles. Paragraph 10 of Sched 4 enables designated CSOs to exercise this power.

Paragraph 11: power to stop vehicle for testing

Under s 67(3) of the Road Traffic Act 1988, a police officer in uniform has the power to stop a vehicle in order for that vehicle to be tested. Under para 11 of Sched 4, this power may also be conferred upon designated CSOs within the relevant police area.

Paragraph 12: power to control traffic for the purposes of escorting a load of exceptional dimensions

This is a particularly interesting aspect of the duties that may be conferred upon designated CSOs for a number of reasons, one of them being that they may exercise the relevant powers given to them outside their police area. Paragraph 12 of Sched 4 empowers designated CSOs to regulate road traffic and pedestrians when escorting vehicles or trailers carrying abnormal loads. They will have the power to direct vehicles and pedestrians to stop, or make vehicles proceed in or keep to a particular line of traffic. Anyone who fails to comply with their directions will commit an offence under ss 35 and 37 of the Road Traffic Act 1988, as if they failed to comply with the directions of a police officer. The maximum penalty for this offence is a level 3 fine (£1,000).

As mentioned above, CSOs given these responsibilities will be able to use their powers outside their normal police area. This is because the provisions state that they may exercise these powers when escorting loads either to or from the relevant police area. This means that the load must either originate within their police area or be destined to go there. Therefore, this power applies to any police area within England and Wales.

The question then arises as to how any offence under s 35 or 37 of the Road Traffic Act 1988 can be prosecuted. There appears to be no mention of any power to issue fixed penalty tickets under these circumstances. This also applies to the power under para 11 above, which involves stopping vehicles. In both cases (and other instances), although the 2002 Act states that CSOs have the power of a constable, this is not strictly accurate. A police officer has powers to deal with certain transgressions against the exercise of his directions. These include the power to issue a fixed penalty notice and the power under s 25 of PACE to arrest in the event of particulars being refused or incorrectly furnished.

Other questions arise regarding these specialised civilian duties, although they apply principally to operational issues. What vehicles will be used by CSOs when performing escort duties? How will they be equipped and to what extent will they be distinguishable from police vehicles?

Paragraph 13: carrying out of road checks

Paragraph 13 of Sched 4 empowers designated CSOs to carry out road checks (or road blocks) under s 4 of PACE. They will have the same powers as the police in performing these duties, which include stopping any vehicle using s 163 of the Road Traffic Act 1988, which is the general power to stop vehicles. They may then ascertain whether the vehicle is carrying a person who has committed, or intends to commit, a serious arrestable offence, a person who is a witness to such an offence or anyone who is unlawfully at large. These powers may only be exercised on the authority of a police superintendent or above, where there are reasonable grounds for believing that the offence concerned is in the serious arrestable category, and where there is reasonable suspicion that the relevant person is, or is about to be, in the locality. In an emergency, this power may be authorised by a police officer below the rank of superintendent. An authorisation may be in force for a period not exceeding seven days, which may operate continuously or intermittently. The person in charge of a vehicle which is stopped under this power is entitled to a written record of the incident. Note that there is no power to search a vehicle or its occupants under s 4 of PACE. Any subsequent searches once the vehicle has stopped must be in accordance with specific powers, and search powers conferred on designated CSOs are limited to those that will be discussed below.

The question arises as to what CSOs will be able to do if they discover a suspect or a fugitive. With regard to the latter, escape from lawful custody is an arrestable offence; therefore, CSOs could rely on their citizen's powers to make an arrest under s 24 of PACE, as the fugitive will be in the act of committing an arrestable offence, namely, fleeing from custody or just being at large. There could be potential difficulties where the suspect *has* committed an arrestable/serious arrestable offence or is *about* to commit such an offence. Section 24 of PACE places certain restrictions on non-police officers where an arrestable offence has been committed or is reasonably suspected of being committed. In either case, the suspect must be guilty of the crime. In the case of a suspect who is about to commit an arrestable/serious arrestable offence, a non-police officer has no power under PACE to make an arrest, but may rely on s 3(1) of the Criminal Law Act 1967. Section 3(1) may also be relied upon when apprehending persons unlawfully at large.

Paragraph 14: cordoned areas

Paragraph 14 of Sched 4 enables designated CSOs to have all the powers of uniformed police officers to give orders, make arrangements or impose prohibitions or restrictions within cordoned areas under the Terrorism Act 2000. Sections 33–35 of the 2000 Act enable a police superintendent or above (or a police officer of lower rank in an emergency) to impose a cordon around a specific area, where it is considered expedient for the purposes of a terrorist investigation. A cordon may be in place for up to 14 days and renewed for a further 14 days. Whilst a cordon is in force, s 36 of the 2000 Act empowers uniformed police officers to do any of the following:

(a) order a person within the cordoned area to leave it immediately;

(b) order a person immediately to leave premises which are wholly or partly in or next to a cordoned area;

(c) order the driver or person in charge of a vehicle to move it immediately from the cordoned area;

(d) arrange for the removal of a vehicle from the cordoned area;

(e) arrange for the repositioning of a vehicle within the cordoned area;

(f) prohibit or restrict access to a cordoned area by pedestrians or vehicles.

It is an offence for a person who fails, without reasonable excuse, to comply with any order, prohibition or restriction mentioned above.[5] The penalty on conviction is a term of imprisonment not exceeding three months and/or a

---

5   Under para 3 of Sched 5 to the 2000 Act, there are further powers that may be attached to imposing a cordoned area, but these only apply to the police.

maximum fine of £2,500. But how can this be enforced by CSOs exercising these powers? There is no express provision for them to require a person's name and address, or the other consequences of a refusal. Probably, it is anticipated that police officers will not be far away from the scene of a cordon and may be able to intervene if such incidents occur.

Paragraph 15: power to stop and search vehicles, etc, in authorised areas

Paragraph 15 of Sched 4 enables more powers held by uniformed police officers under the Terrorism Act 2000 to be conferred upon designated CSOs. These are powers under ss 44(1)(a), (d) and (2)(b) and 45(2) of the 2000 Act, regarding powers of stop and search. These are more limited compared to the full panoply of powers available to the police for whom ss 44 and 45 of the 2000 Act are also available.[6] Those powers which may be exercisable by CSOs are as follows:

(a) to stop any vehicle and search anything in or on that vehicle;

(b) to search anything carried by the driver and any passenger in that vehicle;

(c) to search anything carried by a pedestrian;

(d) to seize and retain anything discovered in the course of the search carried out by him or a police officer.

Note that persons themselves may not be searched by a CSO. This must be confined to searching anything carried by them, such as bags, briefcases and so on. Reasonable force, where necessary, may be used in pursuance of these powers. It should be noted that none of these powers of stop, search and seizure may be exercised by any CSO unless that person is under the supervision of a police officer.

It is an offence for a person to fail to stop for the police, either as the driver of a vehicle or as a pedestrian, or wilfully obstruct them in the exercise of their powers of stop, search and seizure under these provisions. This is punishable by a maximum of six months' imprisonment and/or a fine not exceeding level 5 on the standard scale (£5,000). The question of enforcement should not be difficult here, as CSOs will be in the company of a police officer.

POLICE FORCES PARTICIPATING IN THE CURRENT SCHEME

From 2 December 2002, police forces in England and Wales now have authorisation to train and deploy CSOs within their respective areas. Those participating in this scheme are as follows (those marked with an asterisk are also piloting the 30 minute detention powers for a period of two years): Avon

---

6   The exercise of these powers is subject to an authorisation by an assistant chief constable (or above), or a commander in the Metropolitan or City of London police districts. Initially, they may be for a duration of up to 28 days, subject to ratification or otherwise by the Home Secretary, and are renewable for up to a further 28 days. The additional power that uniformed police officers have under these provisions is the power to search persons rather than just anything carried by them.

and Somerset, Cambridgeshire, Cheshire, Cleveland, Devon and Cornwall,*
Dorset, Durham, Essex, Greater Manchester, Gwent,* Hertfordshire, Kent,
Lancashire,* Leicestershire, Lincolnshire, Merseyside, Metropolitan Police
Service,* Norfolk, Northamptonshire,* Nottinghamshire, South Yorkshire,
Surrey, Sussex, Warwickshire, West Mercia, West Yorkshire* and Wiltshire.

INVESTIGATING OFFICERS (SCHEDULE 4, PART 2)

Introduction

For many years, civilian Scenes of Crime Officers (SOCOs) have been used,
among other things, to gather evidence at crime scenes. However, they do not
possess specific powers in the course of their duties. This is due to be rectified,
by giving them certain police powers, as well as extending this principle to
other classes of civilian investigating officers under the 2002 Act.

According to the government White Paper which preceded the introduction
of the Police Reform Bill in Parliament, the reasons for incorporating specialist
civilian investigators within the extended police family are as follows:

> Money laundering, fraud, intellectual property theft, and other crimes are
> becoming increasingly sophisticated. Information technology and
> communications systems are both the means of crime and its object – and at the
> same time vital investigative tools in the fight against criminals. Too few officers
> currently have the necessary skills to deal with the most complex IT based crime.
> Even with more specialist detectives we will not be able to guarantee an
> adequate capacity in the most specialised fields. We must be able to attract career
> specialists in these areas to work as part of police investigative teams.

> Chief officers can already appoint civilians from these backgrounds, but they are
> unable themselves to exercise police powers necessary to pursue an
> investigation; and they have limited career opportunities open to them.

> Civilian investigators must be able to function as a full member of a police
> investigating team. They should have the capacity to supervise and direct police
> officers in relevant parts of an investigation, acting under the Senior
> Investigating Officer. Given the right skills, such staff should also be able to take
> on the role of Senior Investigating Officer themselves in time. To be fully
> effective, they would need to be given certain police powers. These would
> include, for example, authority to search and seize evidence, to interview
> suspects and witnesses, to execute warrants and to present evidential summaries
> as expert witnesses.

> As a consequence of having these powers, civilian investigators would need to be
> subject to the relevant provisions of PACE 1984 and to police complaints
> procedures. The Government will provide for this and for the powers themselves
> in the Police Bill.[7]

These proposals have now crystallised under s 38 of the Police Reform Act
which, *inter alia*, creates investigating officers whose powers and duties under
Sched 4, Pt 2 are as follows:

---

7   *Policing a New Century: A Blueprint for Reform*, 2001, Cm 5326, The Stationery Office.

Paragraph 16: search warrants

Paragraph 16(1) of Sched 4 enables a designated investigating officer to apply to a justice of the peace for a warrant to enter and search premises. This will apply as if the investigating officer was applying as a constable under s 8 of PACE. These premises must be within the relevant police area where the investigating officer is designated to serve, and any warrant issued must include the investigating officer who applied for it. A designated investigating officer will also have the same powers as the police with regard to the power under s 8(2) of PACE 1984 to seize and retain anything for which a search has been authorised. Investigating officers will also be subject to the following safeguards and procedures as the police, namely ss 15, 16, 19(6), 20, and 21 of PACE.

Paragraph 17: access to excluded and special procedure material

Paragraph 17 of Sched 4 confers powers and duties, under the following provisions of PACE, on designated investigating officers as if they are constables: s 9(1) and Sched 1, 19(6), ss 20, 21 and 22.

Paragraph 18: entry and search after arrest

Paragraph 18 of Sched 4 provides that designated investigating officers shall have the powers and duties of a constable under s 18 of PACE. The main elements of this power are that the police may enter and search premises without a warrant, after the arrest of a suspect. These should be premises occupied or controlled by the suspect who has been arrested for an arrestable offence. This power is for the purposes of obtaining evidence of that offence or another arrestable offence which is connected with or similar to it. This power should not be confused with s 32 of PACE, which enables the police to enter and search any premises in which a suspect was arrested or was in immediately before being arrested. This applies whether or not the premises are occupied or controlled by the suspect, and the offence does not have to be arrestable.

Paragraph 18 also makes designated investigating officers subject to the following provisions under PACE: ss 19(6), 20, 21 and 22.

Paragraph 19: general power of seizure

Paragraph 19 of Sched 4 confers designated investigating officers with the powers and duties under ss 19, 21 and 22 of PACE.

Paragraph 20: access and copying in the case of things seized by constables

Paragraph 20 of Sched 4 provides that where a designation applies to an investigating officer within the relevant police area, s 21(3), (4) and (5) of PACE shall have effect in relation to a designated investigating officer, as if this were a reference to a police officer.

Paragraph 21: arrest at a police station for another offence

Section 31 of PACE provides that:

> Where –
>
> (a) a person –
>
> > (i) has been arrested for an offence; and
>
> > (ii) is at a police station in consequence of that arrest; and
>
> (b) it appears to a constable that, if he were released from that arrest, he would be liable to arrest for some other offence,
>
> he shall be arrested for that other offence.

Paragraph 21(1) of Sched 4 enables this power to be exercised by a designated investigating officer within the relevant police area. Paragraph 21(2) states that the provisions under s 36 of the Criminal Justice and Public Order Act 1994 are also applicable to designated investigating officers within the relevant police area.

Paragraph 22: power to transfer persons into custody of investigating officers

Paragraph 22 of Sched 4 provides that where a person is in police detention for an offence which is being investigated by a designated investigating officer, the custody officer may transfer or permit the transfer of the suspect to that designated investigating officer. The investigating officer shall then be treated as having the suspect in his lawful custody and will be under a duty to prevent his escape, using reasonable force if necessary. The person to whom the suspect is transferred will be subject to the same duties as a police officer under s 39(2) and (3) of PACE.

Paragraph 23: power to require arrested person to account for certain matters

Paragraph 23 of Sched 4 states that a designated investigating officer will have the power of a police officer under ss 36(1)(c) and 37(1)(c) of the Criminal Justice and Public Order Act 1994. This is the power to request a suspect to account for the presence of an object, substance or mark, or for the presence of that suspect at a particular place. The suspect must have been arrested by a police officer, or arrested at a police station by a designated investigating officer (see para 21 above), and be detained within the relevant police area.

Paragraph 24: extended powers of seizure

Paragraph 24 of Sched 4 refers to the extended powers of seizure under Pt 2 of the Criminal Justice and Police Act 2001, and states that the powers exercisable by a constable under these provisions may also be exercised by designated investigating officers. However, these powers are restricted to premises within the relevant police area and things found on such premises. This also applies to the retention of property seized under s 56 of the 2001 Act, which must be seized when the investigating officer was lawfully on any premises within the relevant police area.

DETENTION OFFICERS (DIRECTLY EMPLOYED AND CONTRACTED OUT) (SCHEDULE 4, PART 3)

Paragraph 25: attendance at police station for fingerprinting

Paragraph 25 of Sched 4 gives designated detention officers the power of a constable to require suspects to attend a police station within the relevant police area, in order to have their fingerprints taken (see s 27(1) of PACE).

Paragraph 26: non-intimate searches of detained persons

Section 54 of PACE concerns the power of police officers to carry out non-intimate searches of detained persons. This also empowers police officers to seize and retain, or cause to be seized and retained, anything found during a search. Paragraph 26 of Sched 4 confers these police powers upon designated detention officers within their police area. The provisions under s 54(6C) and (9) of PACE will also apply to designated detention officers as they do to the police. These are the restrictions on the power to seize personal effects and the requirement that these searches must be carried out by a member of the same sex as the detained person. Reasonable force may be used where necessary in the exercise of non-intimate searches of detained persons.

Paragraph 27: searches and examinations to ascertain identity

Paragraph 27 of Sched 4 confers police powers upon designated detention officers within their police area, in order to carry out duties under s 54A of PACE. This enables officers to examine and/or search detained suspects for marks in order to establish their identity or to confirm their connection with an offence. The officers must be of the same sex as the person being searched or examined. This power applies where the suspect does not consent to a search or examination, or it is not practicable to obtain consent, and that person has either refused to identify himself or there are reasonable grounds for suspecting that false information regarding identity has been given. The exercise of this power requires the authorisation of a police officer of at least the rank of inspector before it is carried out. Officers of the same sex as the suspect may take a photograph of any identifying mark discovered in the course of a search or examination of the detained person, whether or not that person consents. Reasonable force may be used where necessary in the exercise of this power.

Paragraph 28: intimate searches of detained persons

Paragraph 28 of Sched 4 enables designated detention officers to carry out intimate searches, within their police area, under s 55 of PACE. This will be subject to the overall provisions under s 55 which include, *inter alia*, the restriction under sub-s (7) that no intimate search should be carried out by a constable of the opposite sex. In this case, that restriction will also apply to detention officers who are designated to use this power. The exercise of this power may involve the use of reasonable force where necessary.

Paragraph 29: fingerprinting without consent

The taking of fingerprints from persons is covered under s 61 of PACE, which also includes the taking of fingerprints without consent. Paragraph 29(a) of Sched 4 gives the powers of a constable to designated detention officers within their police area, in order that they may carry out fingerprinting without the appropriate consent. Paragraph 29(b) makes further provision by stating that s 61(7A)(a) of PACE will apply to designated detention officers as well as to police officers. This provides that before a person's fingerprints are taken at a police station, with or without consent, an officer must inform the suspect that those fingerprints may be the subject of a speculative search. Reasonable force where necessary may be used in the exercise of this power.

Paragraph 30: warnings about intimate samples

Section 62(7A)(a) of PACE makes the following provision regarding intimate samples:

> (7A) If an intimate sample is taken from a person at a police station –
>> (a) before the sample is taken, an officer shall inform him that it may be the subject of a speculative search.

Paragraph 30 of Sched 4 states that such a duty may be discharged by a designated detention officer in a police station within that officer's police area.

Paragraph 31: non-intimate samples

Section 63 of PACE contains provisions regarding the taking of non-intimate samples, with particular reference to taking them without consent. Paragraph 31 of Sched 4 confers police powers on designated detention officers, at police stations within their police area, in order that they may take non-intimate samples without consent, using reasonable force if necessary. Emphasis is placed upon the duty under s 63(6) of PACE to inform the person from whom the sample is to be taken that the appropriate authorisation has been given to take it without consent and the grounds for giving it. The requirement under s 63(8B)(a) of PACE will also apply, namely, that before a non-intimate sample is to be taken, with or without consent, the person should be informed that it may be the subject of a speculative search.

Paragraph 32: attendance at police station for the taking of a sample

Paragraph 32 of Sched 4 states that designated detention officers, at any police station within their police area, shall have the power of a constable under s 63A(4) of PACE. Subject to certain conditions, this is the power to require a person who is not in police detention or custody to attend a police station in order to have a sample taken.

Paragraph 33: photographing persons in police detention

Paragraph 33 of Sched 4 confers the powers of a constable on designated detention officers, at police stations within their police area, with regard to s 64A of PACE. This makes provision for a person detained at a police station to be photographed, with or without their consent; they may also be required to remove anything worn which conceals all or part of the face or head. Reasonable force where necessary may be used in the exercise of this power.

ESCORT OFFICERS (DIRECTLY EMPLOYED AND CONTRACTED OUT) (SCHEDULE 4, PART 4)

Paragraph 34: power to take arrested person to a police station

Under this paragraph, a designated escort officer within the relevant police area will have the power to take a person who has been arrested away from a police station, to either a designated or non-designated police station. This need not be done immediately if the suspect's presence is needed elsewhere for investigative purposes before being taken to a police station. The designated escort officer, taking a person to a police station in the exercise of this power, will be treated as having that person in his lawful custody and is under a duty to prevent that person's escape, for which reasonable force may be used. The latter may also apply, where necessary, in the execution of an escort officer's power to make a non-intimate search of an arrested person in his charge and to seize or retain anything found. This is subject to the restrictions also imposed on the police regarding the seizure of clothing and personal effects, as well as the requirement that these searches must be carried out by a person of the same sex as the detainee.

Paragraph 35: escort of persons in police detention

Paragraph 35 enables custody officers at designated police stations to authorise the transfer of a detainee to other police stations, or to other places, whether or not any destination is within the escort officer's relevant police area. An escort officer will be responsible for ensuring the proper treatment of a detainee once a custody officer has transferred the detained person to that designated person. During this time, the detainee will be in the lawful custody of the escort officer, who has a duty to prevent the detained person's escape, using reasonable force where necessary. The latter will also apply where the escort officer conducts a non-intimate search.

COMPLAINTS AGAINST CIVILIAN OFFICERS

By virtue of s 12(7)(b) of the Police Reform Act 2002, all the above directly-employed civilian officers will fall within the ambit of the Independent Police Complaints Commission in the event of allegations of misconduct. With the provision for possible modifications, the same applies to contracted out civilian detention and escort officers, as discussed below. However, different arrangements will apply to civilians under accreditation schemes, which will also be mentioned later (see Chapter 9, p 67).

POLICE POWERS FOR CONTRACTED OUT STAFF

Section 39 of the Police Reform Act makes provision, where a police authority enters into a contract, for the provision of detention officers and escort officers, and their chief officer of police designates them accordingly. It seems that those who will be providing these civilian officers under contract will be private security companies which, under sub-s (5), must be fit and proper persons to carry out their supervision. The persons running such companies will have to be appropriately licensed by the Security Industry Authority, under the auspices of the Private Security Industry Act 2001, and may even be required by the police authorities to achieve approved supplier status.[8] The civilian officers who are designated to perform these duties will have the same powers and duties as their counterparts, directly employed by police authorities.[9] These are to be found under Sched 4, Pt 3 to the Police Reform Act, in respect of detention officers, and Sched 4, Pt 4, regarding escort officers. A contracted out operative may perform the duties of both a detention officer and an escort officer.

In cases of alleged misconduct on their part, s 39(9) and (10) of the Police Reform Act 2002 enables the Home Secretary to make regulations which are intended to bring them within the ambit of the new Independent Police Complaints Commission, which may be subject to modifications. However, prior to doing this, he is under a duty to consult with those whom he considers to represent the interests of police authorities and chief officers of police (such as the Association of Police Authorities and the Association of Chief Police Officers, respectively), as well as the Independent Police Complaints Commission, in addition to any other persons as he thinks fit. Any designation

---

8 The scope of the Private Security Industry Act 2001 is very wide. Among its numerous regulatory functions is the provision for a voluntary inspection and approval scheme. This will enable suppliers of private security services to apply for recognition as having achieved excellence in the provision of those services. Such recognition may well be insisted upon by many intending to use their services.

9 According to the explanatory notes to the Police Reform Act 2002: 'A number of police forces already contract out aspects of their detention and escort services to the private sector, but employees of companies involved in that work have not had access to relevant police powers.'

under s 39 will no longer have effect if the designated person ceases to be employed by the contractor or if the contract between the contractor and the police authority is either terminated or allowed to expire. Unless the latter occurs, a designation may be renewed.

GENERAL PROVISIONS

As with CSOs, since 2 December 2002, the relevant chief officers can now also commence the recruitment, training and deployment of other designated civilians. It should be noted that with regard to CSOs, both the government and the police service have emphasised that these are an additional resource and are therefore not a substitute for police officers. This assertion is supported by the fact that additional funding has been provided by the government for this purpose.

The use of investigating officers, detention officers and escort officers may fall under the same or similar patterns. However, it seems that the overall use of designated civilians may not only augment the police service in terms of increased size, but many may also serve to release police officers from mainly low-key or routine tasks. In the case of investigating officers, it is intended that they will also bring additional skills into criminal investigations as well as increase the numbers engaged in specialised forms of crime detection.

CHAPTER 9

COMMUNITY SAFETY ACCREDITATION SCHEMES

An introduction to the community safety accreditation schemes was given at the beginning of Chapter 8 (see p 47). Section 40 of the Police Reform Act 2002 introduces this new scheme, which is designed to extend limited police powers to persons already engaged in community safety duties. These include local authority street and neighbourhood wardens, as well as football stewards and security guards within the private security industry, to name but a few. Even persons already exercising official powers, such as Environmental Health officers, may be included.[1]

Where it is considered appropriate, in order to contribute to community safety and security, as well as combating crime and disorder, public nuisance and other forms of anti-social behaviour, a chief officer of police may establish a community safety accreditation scheme (this provision became effective from 2 December 2002). Prior to starting such a scheme, the chief police officer must consult with his or her police authority and every local authority within the relevant police area. The exception to this rule is the Commissioner of Police of the Metropolis, who must consult with the Metropolitan Police Authority, the Mayor of London and every local authority within the metropolitan police district.

Details regarding any accreditation scheme, which is either operating or proposed within a police area, must be included within every police plan submitted by each police authority. The submission of an annual police plan to the Home Secretary is incumbent upon police authorities under s 8 of the Police Act 1996. Initially, this is drafted by its chief officer of police and any changes are made in consultation with him. Section 40(7) of the Police Reform Act states that every police plan must set out whether a community safety accreditation scheme is maintained within the police area in question and whether any changes to that scheme are proposed. If no accreditation scheme exists, there is the requirement to provide details of any proposed scheme. The police plan must also include the extent of any police powers conferred upon designated persons who are employed by that police authority, and the extent to which any existing or proposed accreditation scheme will supplement those arrangements.

The employers of civilians who are part of a community safety accreditation scheme will be expected to supervise them; therefore, sub-s (8) provides that these employers must carry on business related to or within the relevant police area. However, somewhat controversially, the employers of civilians operating within an accreditation scheme will also be expected to handle complaints regarding their alleged misconduct. Considerable concern was expressed regarding this latter provision as the Bill was proceeding through Parliament. It was strongly asserted that accredited civilians should be brought within the remit of the Independent Police Complaints Commission, as are those directly

---

1   *Policing a New Century: A Blueprint for Reform*, 2001, Cm 5326, The Stationery Office.

employed by police authorities, as well as contracted out escort and detention officers.

Section 41 of the Police Reform Act 2002 states the procedures regarding accreditation under community safety accreditation schemes, once a chief police officer has entered into such arrangements with an employer. Accreditation shall not be granted to anyone unless the chief officer of police is satisfied that the employer of that individual is a fit and proper person to supervise him in the carrying out of his accredited functions. It is also a requirement that the individual is a suitable person to be accredited, and is capable of exercising any powers conferred on himself; that person must therefore be adequately trained for this purpose. It is submitted that these provisions generally fall in line with the licensing requirements for certain private security operatives under the Private Security Industry Act 2001. This is one of several examples where the Police Reform Act 2002 and the Private Security Industry Act 2001 are inextricably linked.

Chief police officers may charge appropriate fees for granting accreditations and/or for considering applications for accreditation or any renewals of existing arrangements. Individual operatives must not engage in conduct outside their employment under an accreditation scheme, and an accreditation shall cease if the operative leaves their employment, or accreditation arrangements are terminated or expire.

The powers, in whole or part, that *may* be conferred on accredited civilians are provided under Sched 5 to the Police Reform Act 2002 (see below). As is the case of designated civilians who are directly employed by police authorities, the conferring of powers from the following menu is at the discretion of the relevant chief officer of police, who may also attach restrictions and conditions regarding the exercise of these powers accordingly. It will be apparent that where accredited civilians are given special powers, these are significantly limited compared to those of community support officers (CSOs). One of the distinctions between the two is the omission of the power for accredited civilians to use reasonable force when exercising powers attributable to those of a police officer. Neither are they given the limited detention and other powers held by CSOs, when requests for names and addresses are not complied with. The powers that may be given to accredited persons under Sched 5 follow below.

SCHEDULE 5

Paragraph 1: power to issue fixed penalty notices

An accredited person shall have the power to issue the following fixed penalty notices where he has reason to believe that a person has committed or is committing any of the following offences within the relevant police area:

(a) The power of a constable in uniform to give a person a fixed penalty notice under s 54 of the Road Traffic Offenders Act 1988, in respect of an offence under s 72 of the Highway Act 1835, namely, riding on the footway.

(b) The power of an authorised local authority officer to give a fixed penalty notice in respect of dog fouling under s 4 of the Dogs (Fouling of Land) Act 1996.

(c) The power of an authorised officer of a litter authority to give a fixed penalty notice in respect of litter under s 88 of the Environmental Protection Act 1990.

Paragraph 2: power to require giving of name and address

A further category of offence has been included within the powers of accredited persons, namely, the commission of an offence which appears to the accredited person to have caused injury, alarm or distress to any other person, or the loss of, or any damage to, any other person's property. This category of offence, which clearly encompasses anti-social behaviour, may be subject to certain conditions, which may be specified in the accreditation.

Where an accredited person has reason to believe that any of the offences in this paragraph, or para 1, have been committed within the relevant police area, that person may require the suspect to provide his name and address. Failure to do so constitutes an offence punishable by a fine not exceeding level 3 on the standard scale (currently £1,000). But how is this offence to be enforced? In contrast to Sched 4, Pt 1, para 2(3) and (4), as applies to CSOs, there is no power for an accredited civilian to detain a person who commits this offence, nor is there a power to request the accompaniment of the suspect to a police station. If such a person refuses to provide their name and address or gives obviously false particulars, it seems that this person can simply walk away.

Paragraph 3: power to require name and address of a person acting in an anti-social manner

Where an accredited civilian has reason to believe that a person is acting, or has been acting, in an anti-social manner, that accredited civilian has the power of a constable in uniform to require that person to give his name and address. The power of a uniformed police officer to pursue this course of action can be found under s 50 of the Police Reform Act 2002, and s 1 of the Crime and Disorder Act 1998 provides the meaning as to what constitutes anti-social behaviour. Refusal to provide a name and address or provision of false particulars constitutes an offence under s 50 of the 2002 Act, which is punishable by a maximum level 3 fine. Where this offence has been committed, no special powers of enforcement have been conferred on accredited civilians, so it seems that little can be done to bring the culprits to justice. This would not apply, of course, where a police officer in uniform is exercising the power under s 50. In the event of a refusal to provide a name and address or the provision of false particulars, the general arrest conditions under s 25 of PACE could then be applied. The limited power to detain in such circumstances, or the alternative of escorting the person to a police station, may be given to designated CSOs under Sched 4, Pt 1, para 3 of the Police Reform Act, but this has not been conferred on accredited civilians.

Paragraph 4: alcohol consumption in designated public places

Duly accredited persons within their police area will have the powers of a constable under s 12 of the Criminal Justice and Police Act 2001. This will enable them to direct persons in designated public places not to consume anything reasonably believed to be intoxicating liquor and to confiscate such drink or an open container for such liquor, which may then be disposed of in an appropriate manner. Failure to comply with such a direction, without reasonable excuse, is an offence which must be communicated to the person on whom the requirement is imposed. Any failure to comply is punishable by a maximum level 2 fine (currently £500) and is an arrestable offence under s 24 and Sched 1A of PACE. The latter could be used to overcome the absence of an express provision of enforcement powers on accredited persons in the event of a failure to comply with a direction. As offences that are classed as arrestable enable persons who are not police officers to make arrests, this will also apply to accredited persons. The provisions under this paragraph are almost identical to those under Sched 4, Pt 1, para 5.

Paragraph 5: confiscation of alcohol

These provisions reflect those attributable to designated CSOs under Sched 4, Pt 1, para 6. In the case of accredited civilians, they will also have the powers of constables under s 1 of the Confiscation of Alcohol (Young Persons) Act 1997; but the same problem arises regarding an offence committed under s 1 of the 1997 Act, where the young person fails to surrender intoxicating liquor or provide a name and address. In these circumstances, the police have a power of arrest, but this has been expressly denied to accredited civilians (and designated CSOs). How can an offence under s 1 be directly enforced without the power to do so?

Paragraph 6: confiscation of tobacco, etc

Paragraph 6 is on a par with Sched 4, Pt 1, para 7, which applies to designated CSOs. Paragraph 6 gives accredited civilians within the relevant police area the power of a constable in uniform, under s 7(3) of the Children and Young Persons Act 1933, to confiscate and dispose of tobacco and cigarette papers from under-16 year olds in public places. However, the power to dispose of those items seized must be done in a manner as directed by the relevant employer of an accredited person.

Paragraph 7: abandoned vehicles

These provisions are virtually the same as those under Sched 4, Pt 1, para 10, applicable to designated CSOs. In this instance, they apply to accredited persons who will have the power under s 99 of the Road Traffic Regulation Act 1984 to remove abandoned vehicles or to arrange their removal.

Paragraph 8: power to stop vehicle for testing

Paragraph 8 makes the same provisions as those applicable to designated CSOs under Sched 4, Pt 1, para 11. In this instance, accredited civilians will have the power of a police officer in uniform, under s 67(3) of the Road Traffic Act 1988, to stop a vehicle in order for it to be tested. This power may only be exercised by an accredited person within the relevant police area.

Paragraph 9: power to control traffic for purposes of escorting a load of exceptional dimensions

Unlike other powers that may be conferred upon accredited persons, the powers under *this* paragraph may be applied anywhere in England and Wales, provided the load in question is being escorted to or from the relevant police area. These provisions are virtually the same as those under Sched 4, Pt 1, para 12 in relation to designated CSOs. Also, the same questions arise regarding enforcement of the offences under ss 35 and 37 of the Road Traffic Act 1988 against those who fail to comply with the directions of those escorting these loads.

Supplementary provisions relating to designations and accreditations

Section 42 of the Police Reform Act 2002 makes a number of miscellaneous provisions in respect of the following civilian operatives:

(a) police authority employees who are designated as CSOs, investigating officers, detention officers and escort officers under s 38 of the 2002 Act;

(b) investigating officers employed by one of the service authorities of the National Criminal Intelligence Service or the National Crime Squad under s 38 of the 2002 Act;

(c) contracted out detention officers and escort officers under s 39 of the 2002 Act; and

(d) accredited persons under community safety accreditation schemes under s 41 of the 2002 Act.

Under s 42, anyone exercising powers and duties in reliance on his designation under ss 38 or 39 or accreditation under s 41 must produce his designation or accreditation when requested to do so. Those exercising such powers must wear a uniform, which is determined or approved by the chief police officer who granted the designation or accreditation. Accredited persons will also have to wear a badge, the design of which will be specified by the Home Secretary.

Section 42 then goes on to make provision for chief officers of police and any Director General to modify or withdraw a designation regarding a directly-employed civilian at any time. With regard to contracted out designations and accreditations, there are provisions which stipulate a chief police officer's responsibilities regarding informing the civilian's employer.

The final sub-sections under s 42 are concerned with employers' liability for unlawful conduct in reliance on a designation or accreditation.

RAILWAY SAFETY ACCREDITATION SCHEME

The prime responsibility for policing the rail network throughout this country falls on the British Transport Police Force. In this respect they are a nationwide police force, as their jurisdiction brings them into contact with all police areas. In recognition of this fact, *inter alia*, s 43(1) of the Police Reform Act 2002 makes provision for the Home Secretary to make regulations enabling the chief constable of the British Transport Police Force to institute a railway safety accreditation scheme. Sub-section (2) makes provision that:

> A railway safety accreditation scheme is a scheme for the exercise in, on or in the *vicinity*[2] of policed premises in England and Wales, by persons accredited by the chief constable of the British Transport Police Force under the scheme, of the powers conferred on those persons by their accreditation under that scheme.

The use of the word 'vicinity' is important because this reflects the intention to give accredited persons jurisdiction not only in or on railway property, but also in surrounding areas where troublesome elements may be located.

The regulations that may be made by the Home Secretary are very wide, although before making such regulations, he has a duty to consult with persons he considers to represent the interests of chief officers of police (such as the Association of Chief Police Officers) and police authorities (such as the Association of Police Authorities), as well as local authorities. He must also consult with the chief constable of the British Transport Police Force, the British Transport Police Committee, the Mayor of London and other such persons as he thinks fit. Sub-sections (6) and (7) make it clear that, with two exceptions, accredited persons under this scheme must not be given any powers beyond those stated under Sched 5. The two exceptions are offences under the British Transport Commission Act 1949, namely, trespassing on a railway (s 55) and throwing stones, etc, at trains or other things on railways (s 56).

---

2   Emphasis added.

CHAPTER 10

MISCELLANEOUS PROVISIONS

SECTION 44: REMOVAL OF RESTRICTION ON POWERS CONFERRED ON TRAFFIC WARDENS

Although traffic wardens have certain limited powers to stop vehicles, they do not possess the general power to stop vehicles under s 163 of the Road Traffic Act 1988, as held by the police. Section 44 of the Police Reform Act 2002 amends the Road Traffic Regulation Act 1984, thus conferring on traffic wardens this general power to stop vehicles. This will enable them, *inter alia*, to carry out vehicle escort duties, because they already have the power to direct traffic. The changes effected by s 44 will also enable traffic wardens to stop vehicles in order for them to be tested.

SECTION 45: CODE OF PRACTICE RELATING TO CHIEF OFFICERS' POWERS UNDER CHAPTER 1

Section 45 makes provision for the Home Secretary to issue a code of practice regarding the exercise by chief police officers and Directors General of their powers and duties under Chapter 1 of Pt 4 of the 2002 Act. These codes of practice may be amended, but before they are issued or revised, the Home Secretary is under a duty to consult with the following:

(a) the Service Authority for the National Criminal Intelligence Service;

(b) the Service Authority for the National Crime Squad;

(c) persons whom he considers to represent the interests of police authorities;

(d) the Director General of the National Criminal Intelligence Service;

(e) the Director General of the National Crime Squad;

(f) persons whom he considers to represent the interests of chief officers of police;

(g) persons whom he considers to represent the interests of local authorities;

(h) the Mayor of London;

(i) such other persons as he thinks fit.

The Home Secretary is under a duty to lay these codes of practice before Parliament, as well as any amendments. Also, chief officers of police and Directors General must have regard to these codes of practice when carrying out any function relating to Chapter 1 of Pt 4 of the 2002 Act.

SECTION 46: OFFENCES AGAINST DESIGNATED AND ACCREDITED PERSONS, ETC

Any person who assaults a designated person or an accredited person in the execution of his duty, or anyone assisting such an officer, commits an offence under s 46(1) of the Police Reform Act. This is triable summarily only and punishable by a term of imprisonment not exceeding six months and/or a fine not exceeding level 5 on the standard scale (currently £5,000). Sub-section (2) creates the offence of resisting or wilfully obstructing any of these three classes of person. This is also triable summarily only and subject to a maximum of one month's imprisonment and/or a fine not exceeding level 3 on the standard scale (currently £1,000).

The question of enforcing these offences arises yet again. How can those who commit such acts be brought before the courts? In the absence of an arrest power, can nothing be done directly to bring the culprits to justice? In the case of designated community support officers (CSOs), there may be some safeguards. For instance, they may ultimately be able to draw on their limited powers of detention on the grounds that such conduct amounts to the commission of an offence which appears to have caused injury, alarm or distress, or the loss of, or damage to, property. However, as mentioned earlier, the wording of those provisions indicates that this may not directly apply to a designated CSO who is the victim, in which case, reliance may be placed on another CSO in the immediate vicinity, who may be able to use his detention power as a third party. In any event, the CSO must possess the limited detention power in order to act accordingly. Also, they may be able to draw on their powers as ordinary citizens; however, as mentioned in previous chapters, these may not always be appropriate.

Sub-section (3) makes it an offence to impersonate a designated or accredited person, or for a person to falsely suggest that he is such an operative with intent to deceive. In the case of designated or accredited persons, it will be an offence for any of them to make any statement or act in a way that falsely suggests that they have powers they have not been given. This must also be done with intent to deceive. These offences are triable summarily only and are punishable by a maximum of six months' imprisonment and/or maximum level 5 fine.

SOME OPERATIONAL CONCERNS

Whilst it has been stated that designated and accredited civilians will have access to police radio links, as well as mobile telephones, there is no specific provision under the 2002 Act for them to be equipped with protective clothing, such as stab-proof waistcoats. Hopefully, these will be incorporated with the uniforms that will have to be approved by chief officers of police. Perhaps, most controversially, there is no provision for protective and restraining equipment being issued to these civilians, such as batons, handcuffs, CS gas or pepper spray. Many of these operatives will be working at the sharp end, in terms of law enforcement in public places, including some particularly dangerous areas.

Notwithstanding the intention that they should avoid confrontations with members of the public, anyone with first-hand knowledge of law enforcement will know that this is not always possible.

As a general rule, it appears that only those who hold the status of constable are allowed such protective devices on a regular basis, especially the carrying of batons. This also includes prison officers, who, under s 8 of the Prison Act 1952, have the full powers of a constable in the course of their duties. However, this does not apply to prisoner custody officers working in contracted out prisoner escort services and privately-managed prisons. As observed in Part I of this book, s 8 of the Prison Act has been expressly removed from the ambit of their powers by the Criminal Justice Act 1991.

An important development regarding all classes of civilians with limited police powers occurred on 1 April 2003, when the new Codes of Practice A–E under PACE came into force. These will have to be complied with by the police and all those performing police functions. Also, a new Bill regarding anti-social behaviour is being introduced into Parliament that is likely to affect the work of CSOs in the future.

CONCLUSION

Hopefully, among other things, Part I of this book has illustrated that the concept of the 'extended police family' had been an evolving trend long before the Police Reform Act 2002. However, as this Act gradually comes into force, the effects of this concept will be more widely experienced. It seems that the future policing of this country will be organised increasingly on a multi-agency basis, with the private security industry playing a greater role than ever. In fact, Pt 4, Chapter 1 of the Police Reform Act could be described as the instrument through which a significant part of the private security industry will be directly linked into the police service. However, as much of the above commentary indicates, there may be much consolidation and clarification needed in the years ahead, as various anomalies arising from these new powers become apparent. In the meantime, many will also be watching the progress of the Private Security Industry Act 2001 in its endeavour to regulate the private security industry in this country. The background to this important statute and its wide-ranging provisions will be discussed in the next chapter.

THE BASIC STRUCTURE OF THE EXTENDED POLICE FAMILY

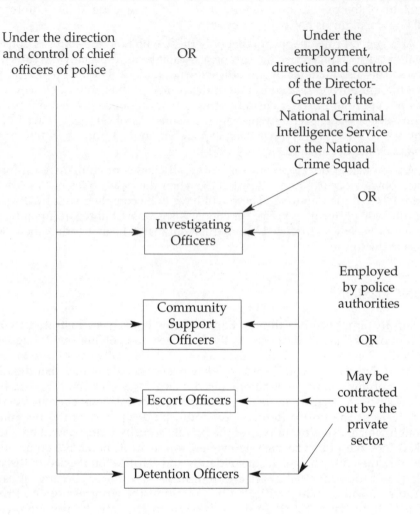

Under the direction
and control of chief   OR
officers of police

Under the
employment,
direction and control
of the Director-
General of the
National Criminal
Intelligence Service
or the National
Crime Squad

OR

Investigating
Officers

Employed
by police
authorities

Community
Support
Officers

OR

Escort Officers

May be
contracted
out by the
private
sector

Detention Officers

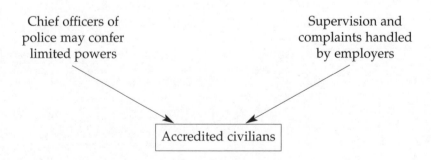

Chief officers of
police may confer
limited powers

Supervision and
complaints handled
by employers

Accredited civilians

PART III: REGULATION OF THE PRIVATE SECURITY INDUSTRY

CHAPTER 11

THE PRIVATE SECURITY INDUSTRY ACT 2001

INTRODUCTION

The Private Security Industry Act ('the Act') was given the Royal Assent on 11 May 2001. The preamble of this statute briefly states that it is 'An Act to make provision for the regulation of the private security industry'. As will be examined in this chapter, this simple statement is likely to have very wide implications in the future, not only for the private security sector but also for many other aspects of commerce and industry. It will also have an impact on the courts by virtue of the specific appeals processes and new criminal offences created under the Act. The principal measures under the Act apply to England and Wales only, and are not yet fully in force, although this process began on 2 April 2003.

As mentioned at the beginning of this book, the role of the private security industry is likely to take on greater importance in the years to come. Traditionally, its main focus has been centred on the protection of assets held by private organisations, but in more recent years, it has become more involved in public protection duties. These include prisoner custody officers employed by the relevant security companies who are responsible for the security at the privately-managed prisons, as well as the prisoner escort service. The security of the privately-managed secure training centres and their escort arrangements is in the hands of 'custody officers' who are also employed by private security companies. More recently, there are 'detainee custody officers' responsible for the security and escort arrangements at the privately-run immigration removal centres; they too are employed by the relevant security companies. Magistrates' court security officers are also from the private security sector, and this includes security officers at the airports. In all these cases, the civilian security personnel mentioned above have been given various statutory powers over and above those normally held by ordinary citizens (and ordinary security officers for that matter).[1] It will have been observed by reading Part I of this book that these powers are focused mainly on the searching of people, including members of the public, as well as various powers to enter property, detain certain vehicles and retain objects in limited circumstances.

---

1   See Part I of this book discussing Part IV of the Criminal Justice Act 1991 regarding prisoner custody officers and magistrates' court security officers; ss13 and 13A of the Aviation Security Act 1982 in respect of airport security officers; Part I of the Criminal Justice and Public Order Act 1994 regarding the security arrangements for secure training centres; and Part VIII of the Immigration and Asylum Act 1999 in respect of immigration removal centres and their escort arrangements. See also the Channel Tunnel (Security) Order 1994 (SI 1994/570) regarding search powers conferred upon civilian staff responsible for operating the Channel Tunnel, as well as the coverage of civilian enforcement officers under the Access to Justice Act 1999.

The private security industry has been subject to a degree of self-regulation for many years. This has been assisted by organisations such as the British Security Industry Association and the Joint Security Industry Council, and many others who are collectively a conglomeration of mainly standard-setting organisations. There are also a number of highly reputable security companies which have set exemplary standards within their own organisations for whom regulation will be a welcome move. In contrast, however, it is the activities of increasing numbers of 'cowboy' operators which have done much to discredit the private security industry and have necessitated regulation at this time.

According to explanatory notes prepared by the Home Office,[2] the private security industry consists of several sectors, but focuses on activities concerned with the following:

- Guarding people and property.
- Wheelclamping.
- Private Investigators.
- Security Consultants.

For about 25 years, various attempts had been made to regulate the private security industry. One of the key figures in this movement, if not the leading figure, was Bruce George, Member of Parliament for Walsall South. Among his numerous attempts to effect statutory regulation of the industry was the Private Security (Registration) Bill published on 31 October 1994. In a White Paper entitled *The Government's Proposals for Regulation of the Private Security Industry in England and Wales*, which was published in March 1999, the Government stated its proposals regarding the statutory regulation of the industry. These proposals are broadly described as follows:

- The exclusion of criminal elements from the industry by introducing a vetting requirement. It is this faction who have tarnished the image of the industry in general by committing offences in breach of the trust placed in them. Vetting will also ensure greater consistency within the industry as a whole.
- Regulation of the industry in order to promote greater consistency and raise general standards within it. This is designed to build upon the progress already made through self-regulation.
- Setting up a *voluntary* inspection scheme enabling companies to achieve recognition of their security services by achieving agreed standards, and subsequently being able to publicise this recognition.

All these objectives are intended to be achieved through the institution of the Security Industry Authority ('the Authority'). There are, however, several key points which should be noted about the Authority and the Act itself. First, not every conceivable activity which falls under the broad heading of private security is currently covered under the Act or the Authority's proposed powers and duties. Only certain designated sectors of the industry will be initially affected, although the list may be changed where necessary in the manner

---

2   *Private Security Industry Act 2001, Explanatory Notes*, 2001, The Stationery Office.

described next. The second main point is that the Act is designed to be flexible insofar as there is much provision for regulations to be made under its auspices. This means that as the overall operation of the Act and the work of the Authority progresses, existing rules may be modified and new rules added where necessary. The Act has to be flexible as it will generally enter uncharted waters, therefore, it was strongly argued in Parliament that provision for such changes must be included in the Act in order to avoid having to pass primary legislation at a later date. For instance, the voluntary inspection and approval of private security providers could be converted into a compulsory scheme if the Home Secretary considers this appropriate in the future. This is in keeping with many other parent Acts which are regulatory by nature.

The new Act, although not very large, is a complex piece of legislation requiring reference to a number of other sources in order to understand its possible effects in the future. This includes extensive reference to parliamentary debate in both Houses as reported in *Hansard,* which may be helpful in indicating the intentions of Parliament behind many important provisions under the Act.[3] Also, reference to Appendix 5 may assist in focusing on the main provisions of this statute.

Section 1: The Security Industry Authority

This section creates and names the Security Industry Authority (sub-s (1)) and defines its powers and duties under sub-s (2) as follows:

- To license those classes of *individuals* working within designated sectors of the private security industry for which licences are required.
- To approve companies supplying relevant security services under a voluntary approval and inspection scheme under the Act.
- To keep under general review the provision of security industry services and other services which involve security operatives.
- To monitor the activities and effectiveness of all those working within the security industry for the purpose of protecting the public.
- To carry out inspections of persons and businesses engaged in security activities which are licensable.
- To conduct inspections of persons registered under the voluntary scheme as approved suppliers of security industry services.
- To set or approve standards of conduct, training and supervision for businesses providing security industry services, or other services involving security operatives, including their employees.
- To make recommendations for the maintenance and improvement of standards in the security industry, or other services involving security operatives.
- To keep the operation of the Private Security Industry Act under review.

---

3   See *Pepper v Hart* [1993] 1 All ER 42, CA and *Three Rivers District Council v Bank of England (No 2)* [1996] 2 All ER 363 regarding the use of *Hansard* in the interpretation of statutes by the courts.

Sub-section (3) makes the wide provision that the Authority may do anything it considers necessary or helpful in the discharge of its functions, and sub-s (4) goes on to state that the Authority may make proposals to the Home Secretary to modify any provision contained under the Act, and to undertake, arrange or support research into the provision of security services. The independence of the Authority from the Crown is provided under sub-s (5); therefore, it will be a non-departmental public body. Schedule 1 to the Act is introduced under sub-s (6), which provides details of the Authority's powers and constitution as follows.

Schedule 1: The Security Industry Authority

Members of the Authority will be appointed by the Home Secretary, including its chairperson. The Act does not state the number of members that may be appointed, but merely provides that this will be determined by the Home Secretary. No member, including the chairperson, may be appointed for more than five years, although appointments may be made for a shorter term. However, they are eligible for re-appointment unless dismissed by the Home Secretary. The grounds for dismissal include: failure without reasonable excuse to carry out duties for a continuous period of three months or absence from three consecutive meetings; being convicted of a criminal offence; being an undischarged bankrupt; failure to comply with the terms of his appointment; or otherwise unable or unfit to perform the functions of a member or the chairperson.

Matters affecting the remuneration, pensions and compensation of members will be determined by the Home Secretary, who will also appoint the Authority's first chief executive. Future chief executives will then be appointed by the Authority, but with the Home Secretary's approval. In 2002, Molly Meacher was appointed as the Authority's chairman (the post-holder's preferred title), and in the same year, John Saunders was appointed as its chief executive. At the time of writing, other members of the Authority have just been appointed, when the Authority was launched on 2 April 2003 (see Appendix 7 for details).

The Authority may establish committees and these may in turn form sub-committees which may consist of one or more non-members of the Authority. Persons on such committees or sub-committees who are not members or employees of the Authority may be paid such remuneration or allowances as the Home Secretary may determine. Schedule 1 also contains a number of procedural provisions which, *inter alia*, include the power of the Authority to regulate its own meetings as well as those pertaining to its committees and sub-committees. The funding of the Authority will consist of payments by the Home Secretary out of money provided by Parliament, and the Authority must not borrow money except with the Home Secretary's consent. Needless to say, the Authority is under a duty to maintain a proper accounting system and must prepare a statement of accounts at the end of the financial year which should be laid before Parliament. This also applies to the Authority's annual report, which should first be submitted to the Home Secretary.

During the passage of the Private Security Industry Bill through Parliament, it was proposed by Lord Cope of Berkeley in the House of Lords whilst in Committee that an obligation for the Authority to consult with the industry as part of its functions should be expressly written into the Bill. This was later withdrawn on the reassurance of Lord Bassam of Brighton, who said that this will occur anyway, as the Authority will consult with the industry in order to hear its views, and may also create committees for this and other purposes (see para 8 of Sched 1 to the Act). He also stated that it was important for at least one representative from the industry to be on the Authority's board, having assured their Lordships earlier that the Home Secretary would not make any regulations without considering the views of both the Authority and the industry.[4]

It should be noted that whilst the Authority is independent of the Crown, it is still a public body and therefore subject to scrutiny under administrative law. It thus, among other things, falls under the list of departments that come within the ambit of the Parliamentary Commissioner (the ombudsman) and it will also be subject to judicial review where appropriate. Members of the Authority are disqualified from being Members of Parliament or the Northern Ireland Assembly. It should also be noted that under s 6 of the Human Rights Act 1998, the Authority, like all public authorities, has a duty to act compatibly with the European Convention on Human Rights.

Notwithstanding the provisions under the Act regarding the Authority's independence from the Crown, some may question this in the light of Sched 1 to the Act. First, all members, including the chairperson, will be appointed by the Home Secretary; secondly, the first chief executive of the Authority will be appointed by the Home Secretary who will have to agree to any subsequent appointment; thirdly, the funding of the Authority will be provided by the Home Secretary from money agreed by Parliament. According to explanatory notes cited during debate in the House of Commons: 'The Security Industry Authority will be self-financing from fees. Funding estimated at £1m is required to establish the Authority and an additional £1.2m to £1.7m to cover a first year operating deficit. These monies will be recoverable from fees. There are also likely to be annually recurring and non-recoverable public expenditure costs of between £0.5m and £0.7m for court costs and possible legal aid involved in any prosecution arising from the new offences created.'[5]

Section 2: Directions etc by the Secretary of State

Under this section, the Authority in carrying out its functions must comply with any general or specific instructions given to it in writing by the Home Secretary, although prior to doing this, the Home Secretary must consult the Authority. The Authority is also under a duty to provide the Home Secretary with such information about its activities as he may request.

Some concern was expressed in both Houses of Parliament regarding the Home Secretary's power under s 2. Such concerns were allayed to some extent by statements that this power would only be used in limited circumstances; for example, due to the Home Secretary's contacts with the police, the civil service and the intelligence services, he may be aware of an undesirable licence

---

4   *Hansard*, House of Lords, 1 March 2001, Cols 1354 and 1359.
5   *Hansard*, House of Commons, Standing Committee B, 1 May 2001, Cols 215–16, *per* Charles Clarke (then Home Office Minister of State).

applicant whose activities may be unknown to the Authority. In such cases, the Home Secretary may then direct the Authority accordingly.[6]

LICENCE REQUIREMENT

Section 3: Conduct prohibited without a licence

Two key phrases are central to this section. They are 'licensable conduct' and 'designated activities'. Licensable conduct under sub-s (1) applies to security work (designated activities) attributable to those categories of people who will need to be licensed by the Authority. These constitute a range of activities defined under this section as well as Sched 2 to the Act, which will be examined in detail below. Designated activities under sub-s (3) refer to specific activities applicable to security operatives which the Home Secretary may apply to licensable conduct in the future. Sub-section (1) also makes the important provision that it will be an offence for a person to engage in any licensable conduct without a licence or, even if they possess one, it will be an offence to engage in any licensable conduct which is not covered under the licence.

A person guilty of an offence under s 1 will be liable on summary conviction to a maximum of six months' imprisonment and/or a fine not exceeding level 5 on the standard scale (currently £5,000). At this point, reference should be made to s 23 of the Act headed 'Criminal liability of directors etc'. This provides that where an offence under any provision of the Act is committed by a body corporate, if it is proved that it was committed with the consent, connivance or neglect of a director, manager, company secretary or similar officer, then that person as well as the company shall be guilty of that offence.

Those categories of people whose security activities will need to be licensed by the Authority are listed under sub-s (2) as follows:

- Directors of security companies; partners of security firms; and security contractors (including sole proprietors).
- Employees of any of the above who are engaged in licensable conduct.
- Agency operatives including directors, partners or employees of the agency or persons who work on a contract basis for the agency.
- Employees who supervise or manage security operatives supplied under contract by security companies, firms, contractors or agencies (for example, sub-contractors).
- Supervisors or managers supplied by agencies to oversee security operatives supplied under contract.
- Directors of security companies and partners of security firms even if not personally engaged in carrying out designated activities. This will apply where any other directors, partners or any employee within the company or partnership engages in licensable conduct.

6   *Hansard*, House of Commons, Standing Committee B, 24 April 2001, Cols 43 and 44, *per* Bruce George, MP.

- In-house wheelclampers and door supervisors as well as their employers, managers and supervisors.

- Other wheelclampers who operate on private land (for instance, those not acting for a landowner but who wheelclamp on their own behalf).

Sub-section (4) provides that employees of end-users of security services, namely those working for organisations to whom such services are supplied under contract, are not required to have a licence if they assume any supervisory or management duties in relation to security staff.

Schedule 2: Activities liable to control under the Act

Section 3(5) of the Act gives effect to Sched 2, which describes the activities that are liable to control under the new legislation. This Schedule is divided into two Parts. Part I is linked to the main part of the Act regarding the activities of security operatives in general, namely: manned guarding, wheelclamping, private investigations, security consultants and key holders. The Home Secretary has the power to modify any of these activities in the future, although this should, among other things, be preceded by consultations with the Security Industry Authority. Part II makes provision for additional controls regarding door supervisors and wheelclampers which could also be subject to modification by the Home Secretary.

Part I: Activities of security operatives

Paragraph 2: Manned guarding

These activities are described under sub-s (1) as:

(a) guarding *premises* against unauthorised access, occupation, outbreaks of disorder or damage;

(b) guarding *property* against destruction, damage or theft (it is submitted that this may include store detectives);

(c) guarding one or more *persons* against assault or personal injury arising from the unlawful conduct of others.

Sub-section (2) states that references to guarding premises against unauthorised access include being wholly or partly responsible for deciding whether or not to admit persons into premises who are seeking entry. According to the Home Office Explanatory Notes,[7] this is designed to ensure that door supervisors are included within this category. It is submitted that this may also apply to sub-s (1)(c), namely guarding persons against assault or unlawfully inflicted injuries even though this is not expressly included.

Sub-section (3) states that guarding by security operatives includes providing a physical presence or carrying out any form of patrol or surveillance in order to deter or discourage something occurring, or to provide information about any such incident.

---

7   *Private Security Industry Act 2001, Explanatory Notes*, 2001, The Stationery Office.

Sub-sections (4), (5) and (6) exclude certain persons from these provisions, thereby enabling them to perform their tasks without licences. These are persons who are confined solely to issuing or checking tickets, or checking that persons seeking entry to premises have invitations or passes allowing admission. Persons who are neither from the former category (ticket collectors, etc) or security operatives, but whose work is incidental to maintaining order and discipline among individuals, are also excluded, as are those who are not security operatives but temporarily perform manned guarding duties in response to a sudden or unexpected occurrence.

Paragraph 3: Immobilisation of vehicles (wheelclamping)

This paragraph defines wheelclamping as 'the immobilisation of a motor vehicle by the attachment to the vehicle, or to a part of it, of an immobilising device ... for the purpose of preventing or inhibiting the removal of a vehicle by a person otherwise entitled to remove it'. However, the provisions under this paragraph do not apply to vehicles on public roads.

Paragraph 4: Private investigators

The activities covered under this paragraph are defined as any surveillance, inquiries or investigations that are carried out in order to obtain information regarding a particular person or their activities or whereabouts, or obtaining information by which property has been lost or damaged. However, the following are excluded:

- activities carried out exclusively for market research purposes. Under this paragraph, 'market research' is defined as including discovering whether a person is a potential customer for any goods or services, or the extent of his or her satisfaction with goods or services already supplied, or obtaining information from any person in order to analyse public opinion on any matter, whether or not this relates to the market for any goods or services;

- activities exclusively carried out for determining creditworthiness;

- barristers and solicitors engaged in their professional activities;

- the professional activities of accountants belonging to any of the following bodies: the Institute of Chartered Accountants (in England, Wales, Scotland and Ireland), the Association of Chartered Certified Accountants, the Chartered Institute of Management Accountants and the Chartered Institute of Public Finance and Accountancy;

- the professional activities of broadcasters and journalists as well as obtaining information relating to literary, artistic or reference works intended for publication in the public domain;

- activities carried out exclusively by reference to published works or to registers or other records that are open to the public, or which are kept by the person by whom or on whose behalf the activities are carried out or to which that person has access;

- activities carried out with the knowledge or consent of the person who is the subject of the investigation;

- activities of a person who conducts any inquiries or investigations which are merely incidental to the carrying out of activities but which are not those of a security operative.

Paragraph 5: Security consultants

This paragraph defines security consultancy as giving advice regarding the taking of security precautions in relation to any risk to property or to the person, or the acquisition of any services which involve the activities of a security operative. There are three express exceptions to this definition which mean that the following will not have to be licensed: first, persons who provide legal or financial advice; secondly, members of the relevant accountancy bodies as listed above under para 4; and thirdly, persons who provide training for security operatives.

Paragraph 6: Key holders

This paragraph contains a definition of what constitutes a 'lock' for the purposes of the Act, namely 'a lock or similar device (whether operated mechanically, electronically or otherwise) that is designed or adapted for protecting any premises against unauthorised entry, or for securing any safe or other container specifically designed or adapted to hold valuables'.

It then goes on to define key holding as 'keeping custody of, or controlling access to, any key or similar device for operating (whether mechanically, electronically or otherwise) any lock'. There are two main exceptions to this definition who therefore do not have to be licensed: first, those whose activities are concerned with the sale of premises or other property; secondly, those who are not security operatives but who hold a key or other device for obtaining entry to premises. This will include those who look after the homes of their neighbours and hold their keys for this purpose (see the debate on this issue below).

Part II: Activities subject to additional controls

Paragraph 7: General

This paragraph, which begins by stating that any reference to designated activities in the Act that are subject to 'additional controls,' means those activities which are covered in Part II. It then goes on to state that the Home Secretary has the power to add or remove any activities to these provisions which impose additional controls.

Paragraph 8: Door supervisors etc for public houses, clubs and comparable venues

Those subject to additional controls by virtue of this paragraph are defined as persons engaged in manned guarding performed in relation to licensed premises when open to the public.

Paragraph 9: Immobilisation of vehicles (wheelclamping)

This very briefly states that wheelclamping is a further category of security activity which is subject to additional controls.

An examination of the provisions so far will disclose that most in-house security activities are precluded from the licensing regime, the exceptions being in-house door supervisors and wheelclampers, which will be discussed later. Some concern was expressed in both Houses of Parliament regarding the exemption of most in-house security activities from the ambit of the Authority's licensing powers. In the House of Lords, Lord Thomas of Gresford, when proposing an amendment to the Private Security Industry Bill which would have included in-house security within the licensing regime, made the following comment:

> I moved a similar amendment during the Bill's Committee stage. The answer that I received then was that the amendment was unnecessary because it would involve double vetting of security staff; a company will vet its staff, but requiring a licence from the authority would be an uncalled for double precaution.[8]

His Lordship then went on to state that there was a potential loophole created by the exclusion of in-house security personnel and added:

> My concern is that should it so happen that firms seek to circumvent the Bill simply by employing unlicensed staff when in ordinary circumstances they would have employed licensed staff through a company – if that loophole exists – the authority will quickly bring the situation to the attention of the Secretary of State, who will remedy it, if necessary through regulations ...[9]

Lord Bassam of Brighton, Parliamentary Under-Secretary of State for the Home Office, later made the following statement on this issue:

> As the noble Lord said, in the White Paper we envisaged that 'in-house' manned guards, along with other groups that are the subject of the amendment, should be included in the licensing regime. However, after careful consideration we decided not to include them at this stage because we concluded that requiring all in-house manned guards to undergo effectively two vetting processes – by the employer and the authority – would add a largely unnecessary layer of bureaucracy to business. In my view, there is bureaucracy and unnecessary bureaucracy, and we believe that the proposal would contribute to the latter ... When the Security Industry Authority is established, it will have a duty to keep the industry and the operation of legislation under review. I have no doubt that the authority will receive arguments about in-house staff, and the Government will be very happy to listen to those views in due course ...[10]

In the House of Commons, similar concerns were expressed regarding the exclusion of most in-house security activities from the licensing requirements under the Bill. Mr Charles Clarke, then Minister of State at the Home Office, made the following reply:

8   *Hansard*, House of Lords, 5 March 2001, Col 13.
9   *Ibid*.
10   *Ibid*, Col 14.

The White Paper envisaged that in-house manned guards would be included in the licensing regime but, after lengthy and detailed consideration, we decided not to do that at this stage. We concluded that to require all in-house manned guards to undergo two vetting processes – by the employer and by the authority – could add a further burden of bureaucracy on to business. It would also have the effect of adding enormously to the already large number of people whom the authority will need to license when it is up and running – the estimated range from between 300,000 to 350,000 people – and we felt that it was important to establish the authority and to clarify its aims without giving it such an enormous amount to bite off that it might make its task more daunting. The Bill regulates some in-house staff, particularly door supervisors and wheelclampers. We focused on those particular groups because they can exercise considerable influence and power over people who might be young or vulnerable, or both. However, the White Paper generated substantial representations that led us to conclude that it was reasonable, at least for the time being, for companies to continue to satisfy themselves about the probity of their employees and potential employees. A distinction must be drawn between such situations and those in which services are provided under contract and the person hiring the services must place a greater degree of trust in the probity of the hired staff ... We understand the argument that has been advanced to the effect that not licensing in-house manned guards could lead to companies switching from contract staff to in-house staff because it will be cheaper and that will, in turn, lead to deteriorating standards in those companies. That is a serious argument for including in-house staff. I have no doubt that the Security Industry Authority will be receiving such arguments and that it will pay close attention to them as part of its general duty to keep the industry and the operation of legislation under review. The Government will listen carefully to arguments from the authority, and that is one of the reasons why we have structured the first part of the Bill as we have. It will ensure that such issues are kept under review.[11]

The above comments by the then Minister of State disclose a number of other interesting features regarding the proposed future operation of the Act, as well as the private security industry itself. A point was later made during the proceedings by Mr Ronnie Fearn MP, who said:

I want to comment on a phrase used by the Minister. He said that he thought that between 300,000 and 350,000 personnel were involved. So far, during debates on the Bill, we have heard figures of 200,000, 250,000 and now 350,000. It seems impossible and amazing that we do not know how many people work within the business that we are about to regulate. Perhaps we will find out when the regulation comes about ...[12]

It is submitted that this is one of the reasons for regulation at the present time. The private security industry is extremely diverse and difficult to quantify in terms of its personnel. Certain sectors of the industry experience a high turnover of staff, which is also subject to a significant degree of casualisation. This is exacerbated by the practice of 'moonlighting' where persons already employed perform part-time security duties in addition to their regular

---

11 *Hansard*, House of Commons, Standing Committee B, 24 April 2001, Cols 67–68.
12 *Ibid*, Col 70.

employment. Also, a large proportion of security staff are employed in-house (that is, companies employ their own security employees as members of staff rather than contracting them in from security companies), which adds further difficulties in accurately assessing the number of private security operatives in this country. Among many other things, the establishment of the Authority may well provide a clearer overall picture of the industry in the future.

Other issues regarding s 3 of the Act were debated whilst the Bill was proceeding through Parliament. One point was raised by Mr John Bercow MP, who said:

> Let us consider, for example, someone who is unpaid or someone who is paid a small sum to look after the door at a local event, perhaps *in extremis*, in circumstances that could not have been envisaged beforehand. The sum involved might be small – £5, for example – but would such a circumstance be covered? That is not entirely clear. How will the Bill affect people who may perform security-related activities on a one-off basis and without payment. In another place, my noble Friend Lord Cope of Berkeley cited the example of someone acting as a door supervisor at a charity jumble sale. Would such a person be caught by the provisions of the Bill ? ... How will churchwardens and other volunteers who might have a security role be affected? It may be that, at the event in question, their exclusive duty – not even their main one – is to act in a security capacity, even though their normal role is that of churchwarden or another similar, or dissimilar function. In such circumstances, would the exemptions in schedule 2 be sufficient to stop them being affected? How would the provisions of schedule 2 ... relate to someone who held his or her neighbour's house keys and otherwise looked after his or her neighbour's house while that neighbour went on holiday ? Would such a person be covered by the existing wording? ... We need to be sure that such a person would not be caught by the provision, because that person might have a primary and even exclusive responsibility for guarding that property for the period in question ...[13]

In response, Mr Charles Clarke acknowledged that this was 'intended to protect volunteers and others from regulations, and to protect small businesses from disproportionately costly legislation',[14] but went on to say:

> First, I will deal with people who might undertake relevant activities but are not remunerated, such as churchwardens – an example that the Hon Member for Buckingham mentioned – someone who is working unpaid for a school, or the neighbour who is a key holder. Such people will not be regulated. The Bill is directed at people who provide services under contract, or who are employed in-house such as door supervisors and wheelclampers. Such matters are covered in [section 3 and] schedule 2. The licensing arrangements do not apply to the majority of people who undertake the activities of a security operative on a no-contract or reward-free basis: the main exception is wheelclampers ... the Bill also does not apply to people who carry out security-related activities that are incidental to their main employment, such as people who work with schools, churches or registered charities. However, if a school, church or charity were to hire security operatives under contract, it is right that it should expect the company contracted to have been vetted to a national standard and licensed. If the security operatives used were employed in-house, they would be exempted from the licensing requirement and it would be the organisation's responsibility

---

13   *Ibid*, Col 59.
14   *Ibid*, Col 60.

to vet its own staff ... The only exception to the general principle that I have described relates to the special case of wheelclamping. In that case only, the [section] extends regulatory controls to others, such as landowners and those acting on their behalf, where they do not have a licensed contractor, but do their own clamping and charge a release fee ... I wish to make it clear that volunteers who engage on wheelclamping that involves a release fee would need a licence.[15]

On the issue of small businesses, Mr Clarke went on to say:

Regulation must be consistent and it would be confusing and difficult to administer the exemption of small businesses from licensing. However, most importantly, that would exempt some of the businesses that are the source of much public disquiet that the Bill seeks to address. It is generally not the big reputable firms that harass the public by employing violent or abusive door supervisors, or who demand money with menaces from innocent wheelclamped motorists, but small companies, organisations and individuals who are the furthest from a reputable and non-criminal practice and must be regulated.[16]

Prior to departing from debate on what was then cl 3 of the Bill (now s 3 of the Act), Mr Clarke made the following statement regarding IT consultants in response to concerns that they would be caught within the ambit of the Bill. Referring to an earlier statement he made during the Second Reading of the Bill, Mr Clarke repeated: '... I am happy to make it clear that we do not currently intend to bring the information security industry within the scope of the new licensing regime established by the Bill.'[17] In response to continuing concerns from the IT industry, the matter emerged yet again during the Report Stage of the Bill. Mr Clarke then gave the following reassurances:

The term 'security consultant' means someone advising on the taking of security precautions in relation to any risk to property or to the person. The licensing requirements under that definition will, as with all parts of the Bill, be brought into effect in due course by implementing regulations, and those regulations will need to specify exactly which security consultancy activities are licensable. Activities that are not specified will not be licensable. It is our fundamental principle to ensure that the Bill is targeted at those specialist providers of security services whom we have indicated we want to regulate, and that the provisions do not inadvertently catch groups that are not relevant to our policy aims. I tried to put the position of IT security consultants in relation to the Bill beyond doubt on Second Reading and in Committee ... I should like the IT industry to take careful note of what I said in Committee: I should like it to be clear to the industry ... that the information security consultancy industry is not under threat of licensing at a future date under this Bill.[18]

15　*Ibid*, Cols 60–62.
16　*Ibid*, Col 62.
17　*Ibid*, Col 79.
18　*Hansard*, House of Commons, Official Report, Parliamentary Debates, 8 May 2001, Cols 51–52.

Section 4: Exemptions from licensing requirement

This section makes provision for the Home Secretary to make regulations whereby certain persons may be exempted from the licensing requirements under the Act and will therefore not commit an offence under s 3. The circumstances under which this may apply are where a security operative is already subject to vetting arrangements which are equivalent to those introduced by the Act. (The power to decide whether alternative vetting arrangements regarding employers are sufficient, may be delegated to the Authority.) In either case, the Home Secretary must be satisfied that the vetting arrangements offer equivalent public protection to those under the Act's licensing regime. Section 4 also states that it will not be an offence under s 3 if any security operative, whether a director, partner, or employee, carries out security activities whilst a pending licence application is with the Authority, provided the following conditions apply:

- the licence applied for covers those activities and that such a licence has not previously been refused; and
- the organisation, or as the case may be, the employer, is registered under s 14 as an approved provider of security industry services (see below for the commentary on s 14); and
- the Authority has authorised that organisation or person to carry out security activities in the pending application whether the applicants are directors, partners or employees.

These provisions also apply to agency staff.

Section 5: Offence of using unlicensed security operative

This section creates the criminal offence of providing the services of an unlicensed security operative to another. This is more serious than an offence under s 3 where a person actually engages in licensable conduct without a licence. The gravity of an offence under s 5 is reflected in the maximum penalties on conviction which are six months' imprisonment and/or a fine not exceeding £5,000 on summary conviction, or five years' imprisonment and/or an unlimited fine when tried on indictment. This offence is therefore triable either way and, by virtue of the potential five years' imprisonment, constitutes an arrestable offence under s 24 of the Police and Criminal Evidence Act 1984.

Unlike an offence under s 3, there are special defences under s 5 (with the exception of s 4 which also applies to s 5). The first is that it will be a defence for the accused to show that he did not know, and had no reasonable grounds for suspecting that the security operative in question was unlicensed; the second is that the accused took all reasonable steps to ensure that the unlicensed security operative in question would not engage in any licensable conduct; the third is where security services are supplied by a person who is exempt from the licensing requirement under s 4, as discussed above. The provisions under s 23 will also apply to both corporate and individual criminal liability where appropriate.

Section 6: Offence of using unlicensed wheelclampers

A further new criminal offence is created under the Act, namely the offence of using unlicensed wheelclampers. Section 6 provides that it will be an offence for a person who is the occupier of any premises to permit an unlicensed person to wheelclamp any vehicle where a licence to do so is required. The same special defences applicable to s 5 also apply to s 6, namely that the accused did not know, and had no reasonable grounds for suspecting that the individual was not the holder of a licence covering wheelclamping; or that the accused took all reasonable steps to ensure that the unlicensed wheelclamper would not engage in any such activity. The further defence also applies here where the wheelclamper may be exempt from the licensing requirement by virtue of s 4. The same maximum penalties apply under s 6 as in s 5, namely six months' imprisonment and/or a fine not exceeding £5,000 when tried summarily, or five years' imprisonment and/or an unlimited fine when tried on indictment. This triable either way offence is also arrestable and can be committed by a corporate body as well as by individuals, as stated under s 23. It should be noted that under s 25 of the Act, the definition of 'premises' includes any place whatever, whether or not occupied as land (as well as any vehicle or movable structure), and a 'motor vehicle' is defined as being a mechanically propelled vehicle or a vehicle designed or adapted for towing by a mechanically propelled vehicle.

LICENSING FUNCTIONS OF THE AUTHORITY

Section 7: Licensing criteria

Section 7 places a duty on the Authority to publish the criteria that it will use in deciding whether or not to grant, revoke or modify licences. This may be amended where appropriate and must be published accordingly. In setting the original or any revised criteria, the Authority must ensure that this results in fit and proper persons being licensed to engage in licensable conduct. Also, the Authority has a discretion to include any criteria which it considers appropriate to ensure that applicants have the training and skills necessary for the relevant licensable conduct; there are further discretionary powers available to the Authority which enable it to include any other criteria it thinks fit, and may also set out different criteria in relation to different types of licences as well as establishing different criteria regarding their renewal. Although the provisions under s 7 appear to give the Authority very wide discretionary powers, under sub-s (5), there is the proviso that the Home Secretary must approve of any criteria that the Authority wishes to apply. The Authority is also under a duty to bring all published criteria to the attention of those likely to be affected by it, and in such a manner as the Authority considers appropriate.

Section 8: Licences to engage in licensable conduct

Section 8 is yet a further illustration of the very flexible nature of the Act. As mentioned above, this is necessary because of the scope and complexity of the private security industry. Odd though it may seem, its full size and scope may not be apparent until it is regulated! Parliament has therefore included many provisions for the making of regulations under the Act in order to deal with unforeseen developments.

Section 8 begins by stating that the Authority has the power to grant licences. In turn, an application for a licence must be in the form, and accompanied by such information, as prescribed in regulations and the Authority must apply the criteria as described under s 7 above when deciding whether or not to issue a licence. The Authority may refuse to grant a licence under the following circumstances:

- until it is satisfied as to the identity of the applicant, which must be done in the prescribed manner;

- until the applicant has supplemented the application with any further information requested by the Authority;

- until the Authority has been able to carry out any further enquiries regarding the applicant.

A licence fee is payable by the applicant, although the amount is not stated in the Act. However, during debate on the Bill in Parliament, it was stated that the fee would be around £40, although ultimately this will be prescribed by the Home Secretary. Sub-section (8) provides that a licence will normally be valid for three years, although different validity periods may be made by the Home Secretary by order. Licences issued by the Authority must be in accordance with prevailing regulations regarding their form, content and conditions, although further conditions may also be attached to the licence at the Authority's discretion. Some of the conditions that may be prescribed under regulations by the Home Secretary, as well as the additional conditions that may be imposed by the Authority, are listed below under the commentary on s 9.

Section 9: Licence conditions

Section 9 makes provision for some of the conditions that the Home Secretary may prescribe for the issue of licences, as well as additional conditions that may be imposed by the Authority. These are as follows:

- conditions relating to training, registration and insurance which the licensee is to undergo or to maintain while the licence is in force;

- conditions as to the manner in which the licensee is to conduct specified activities as a security operative;

- conditions regarding the production and display of the licence;

- conditions imposing obligations as to information the licensee is obliged to provide to the Authority from time to time;

- conditions of any other nature that the Home Secretary or the Authority may prescribe.

Sub-section (3) focuses on designated security activities that are subject to additional controls, namely those relating to door supervisors and wheelclampers. This sub-section states that those conditions mentioned above apply to those actually engaged in door supervision and wheelclamping as well as those who employ them. In other words, both classes of individuals are regarded as 'licensees'.

Another new offence is created under the Act, namely contravention of the conditions of any licence. This is triable summarily only and subject to a maximum penalty of six months' imprisonment and/or a fine not exceeding £5,000. Where applicable, an offence under s 9 may also be committed by an individual as well as a corporate body (see s 23). However, it will be a defence for the accused to show that all due diligence was exercised to avoid a contravention of the conditions of a licence.

Section 10: Revocation and modification of licences

Section 10 empowers the Authority to give notice in writing to a licensee in order to modify, suspend or revoke his or her licence, including any conditions attached to that licence. When deciding on any such course of action, the Authority is under a duty to apply the criteria applicable under s 7 (see above). Although not expressly mentioned, it is presumed that the Authority's powers may also extend to refusing to renew a licence.

Section 11: Appeals in licensing matters

Where an application for a licence is refused (presumably including a refusal to renew an existing licence), or a licence has been granted but subject to additional conditions imposed on the Authority's discretion (see ss 8 and 9 above), or a licence is revoked or modified (which presumably includes being suspended), the applicant or the holder of the licence may appeal to the relevant magistrates' court against the Authority's decision. This is subject to a time limit of 21 days from the date on which the decision was first notified to the appellant. If either the person bringing the appeal or the Authority disputes the decision of the magistrates' court, an appeal may then be made to the Crown Court. Both courts are under a duty to determine the case in accordance with the criteria currently in force under s 7.

At first sight, the Crown Court appears to be the final appellate route for such appeals, but it is submitted that in appropriate cases, an appeal may be made by either party to the Divisional Court by way of case-stated, or an application may be made for judicial review.

During the stages of an appeal based on the refusal of a licence or a revocation (or presumably a suspension), the licence shall remain in force during any such period as the court may direct. These provisions are virtually identical to those under s 18 which state the route by which appeals against refusals to grant approved contractor status may be directed.

Section 12: Register of licences

The Authority has a duty to keep a register of all persons licensed under the Act which must contain the following particulars:

- the licence holder's name;
- an address for the holder which conforms to the prescribed requirements;
- the renewal date of the licence;
- the terms and other conditions of the licence.

The Authority must allow access to the register by members of the public and other persons as it thinks fit, who may also take copies of any part of it. The Authority may charge a fee for any of these services. It also has a duty to ensure that sufficient publicity is given to any modification or revocation of a licence so as to bring this to the attention of those likely to be interested in it.

Section 13: Licensing at local authority level

Section 13 further exemplifies the Act's emphasis on designated activities which are subject to additional controls, in this case door supervisors. Under this section, the Home Secretary may by order make provision for local authorities to carry out the Authority's functions (except those under s 7) in respect of the grant, modification and revocation of licences for door supervisors. An order under s 13 allows the Home Secretary to place conditions and requirements on local authorities exercising the Authority's relevant licensing functions, and to provide for any of the functions given to a local authority to be conducted concurrently by the Authority. An order may also enable a local authority to retain any licence fee paid to it, and the Home Secretary must consult the Authority before delegating any of its licensing functions to local authorities. The same route of appeal applicable to licensing decisions by the Authority will also apply to decisions made by any local authority (see s 11). Any local enactments relating to local registration schemes involving security operatives may be amended or repealed by the Home Secretary when the Act itself comes into force, or when any delegation of licensing functions occurs under s 13.

APPROVED CONTRACTORS

Sections 14–18 establish a voluntary system of inspection on the part of providers of security services. Those who meet the agreed standards may be registered as approved, and therefore advertise themselves accordingly.[19]

Section 14: Register of approved contractors

The Authority is under a duty to keep a register of approved suppliers of security services which must include the following:

- the person's name;
- the person's address which meets the prescribed requirements;
- the person's services which have been approved;

---

19 *Private Security Industry Act 2001, Explanatory Notes*, 2001, The Stationery Office.

- the renewal date of the approval;
- the conditions of the approval.

Members of the public must be allowed access to the register, for which the Authority may charge a fee for inspecting or copying any part of it. The Authority is also under a duty to sufficiently publicise any modification or withdrawal of an approval so as to bring it to the attention of any persons who are likely to be interested in it.

Section 15: Arrangements for the grant of approvals

This section contains the procedures by which the Authority shall grant approved status to the relevant providers of security industry services who apply for such recognition and who meet the required standards. The Authority is under a duty to secure such arrangements and to ensure the following:

- allow for an approval to be granted for some or all of the services offered by the supplier;
- attach conditions to an approval;
- enable a person to refuse an approval if it differs from the terms sought in the proposal;
- make provision for handling complaints and disputes which are not disposed of by the approved supplier's own complaints procedures;
- provide that an approval will have effect for three years (subject to renewal), or such period as the Home Secretary may specify by order;
- provide for the modification or withdrawal of approvals;
- ensure that an approval is granted only if the conditions under sub-s (3) are fulfilled. These conditions are that the Authority must be satisfied that the applicant for an approval:
  - (1) will comply with such technical and other requirements as may be prescribed in providing the services in question. This may be the result of expert opinion being sought in accordance with regulations that may be made;
  - (2) will satisfy any other requirements that may be prescribed. This may also be the result of the Authority seeking expert opinion under regulations;
  - (3) will continue to comply with any conditions that the Authority is proposing to impose both now and in the future;
  - (4) is a fit and proper person to be granted an approval in respect of supplying specific security services.

Sub-section (5) includes two further requirements that may be contained within the conditions in an approval. The first is the requirement to provide information as specified under the terms of the condition, the second is that expert opinion may be used in framing any requirements. The Authority is permitted to enforce any requirement to provide information on a person applying for approval, and persons already granted or seeking an approval, or applying for a modification of one in whole or part, must pay the Authority a fee as may be prescribed.

Section 16: Right to use approved status

Contractors who have been given approved status may advertise this fact. During debate in Parliament, it was mentioned that this may be done by showing a logo or emblem on their stationery, for instance. Under s 16, the Authority may therefore approve the way in which approved contractors hold themselves out to be so registered. It will be an offence for a person to falsely claim to be registered under s 14 as an approved provider of any security industry services. This includes claiming approved status which has not been awarded, or misrepresenting the terms under which the approval has been given. Provision has been made under sub-s (4) to prevent a person evading prosecution by falsely claiming approval whilst not claiming to be on the register of approved contractors. The maximum sentences for any of these offences are restricted to financial penalties only. If tried summarily before magistrates, the maximum fine is £5,000, whereas an unlimited fine will apply if the case is tried on indictment before the Crown Court. Section 23 also applies here with regard to both individual as well as corporate criminal liability.

Section 17: Imposition of requirements for approval

This section could have very wide-ranging implications not only for the private security industry but also the wider commercial sector. Section 17 enables the Home Secretary to make regulations that would transform the voluntary scheme for approved suppliers into a compulsory one. If this is done, only specified security services or activities may be provided. If this scheme is made compulsory, it will be a criminal offence for a person to provide specified security services who is not an approved contractor, or if they are approved, it will be an offence to contravene any conditions attached to the approval. The maximum sentence for either offence will be restricted to a financial penalty only, namely a fine not exceeding £5,000 when tried summarily or an unlimited fine when tried on indictment. If the Home Secretary uses this power, he may insert conditions regarding the handling of complaints in respect of individual firms or companies, and may make those arrangements necessary for any compulsory approval scheme to be introduced.

Section 18: Appeals relating to approvals

The route of appeal against refusals to grant approved contractor status, or a decision to modify or withdraw it, or attach conditions to the approval is virtually identical to that under s 11 above regarding appeals relating to licensing matters.

ENTRY, INSPECTION AND INFORMATION

As the explanatory notes to the Act state: 'Sections 19–22 relate to the Authority's powers of entry and inspection, and to its ability to demand the production of information.' These provisions will now be discussed.

Section 19: Powers of entry and inspection

The work of the Authority would, of course, be of little effect if there were no means by which its powers and duties could be enforced. Section 19 therefore creates a system of enforcement whereby persons appointed in writing by the Authority (henceforward called 'inspectors') may enter premises owned or occupied by persons under certain conditions. The powers of these inspectors and the limitations on those powers are as follows:

- the premises in question must *not* be occupied *exclusively* as a private dwelling for residential purposes;
- the owner or occupier of the premises concerned must be a 'regulated person' meaning:
  - (a) the holder of a licence which has been granted under the Act;
  - (b) a person who engages in licensable conduct but is unlicensed;
  - (c) an approved supplier of security services subject to any conditions attached to the approval, but only if a compulsory approval scheme is in force;
  - (d) a provider of security services who is not approved, but only if a compulsory approval scheme is in force;
- an inspector entering premises must do so at a reasonable hour;
- an inspector exercising this power of entry has a duty to comply with the following requirements under the Act and must:
  - (a) state the purpose for which this power is being exercised if requested by any person present on those premises;
  - (b) show the written authorisation by the Authority for the exercise of the power if requested;
  - (c) produce evidence of his or her identity if requested;
  - (d) compile a record covering the main points regarding the entry in question, namely the date and time it occurred, the period the inspector remained on the premises and the conduct of the inspector while there;
  - (e) provide a copy of the above record to any person on the premises at the time of the entry, if requested;
- an inspector may require anyone who appears to be a 'regulated person' to produce documents or other information in connection with:
  - (a) any past or present licensable conduct, or any conditions attached to a licence;
  - (b) the provision of any security industry services;
  - (c) *any* conditions attached to approved contractor status.

It will be a criminal offence if a person intentionally obstructs an inspector or fails, without reasonable excuse, to provide documents or other information required during an inspection. This offence (which is also subject to s 23) is triable summarily only and punishable by a maximum of six months' imprisonment and/or a fine not exceeding level 5 on the standard scale (currently £5,000). These penalties also apply to anyone found guilty of making unauthorised disclosure of information obtained in the course of an inspection. This will apply not only to the inspectors themselves, but to anyone working for the Authority who has access to this information. The definition of 'authorised disclosure' is strictly limited to the provisions under sub-s (6), which state that it must be confined to disclosure enabling the Authority to carry out any of its functions under the Act, or for the purpose of any criminal proceedings.

At first sight, there appears to be a loophole in the inspection provisions in so far as they seem to have excluded approved suppliers of security industry services under the *voluntary* scheme from the ambit of regulated persons. If that is the case, how will the Authority ensure that approved suppliers under the voluntary scheme are complying with the terms of their approval as well as any conditions that may be attached? It is submitted that the answer may be that approved suppliers will also be licensed as security operatives; therefore, they will be regarded as regulated persons by virtue of that definition, thus enabling inspectors to exercise their entry and inspection powers. Also, what if a person falsely holds his or herself out to be an approved supplier of security industry services under a voluntary scheme? It is submitted that inspectors wishing to investigate those activities may rely on the fact that such persons will also be subject to a licensing requirement and this could enable them to exercise their entry and inspection powers accordingly.

Section 20: Guidance as to exercise of power of entry

This section places a duty on the Authority to prepare and publish guidance regarding the manner in which its inspectors should exercise their powers of entry as well as their subsequent conduct after entering the premises in question. This may be revised when necessary, and in both instances, the Authority must publish this guidance in a manner which will bring it to the attention of those likely to be affected by this information.

Section 21: Access to enhanced criminal records certificates

An important part of the Authority's vetting process regarding the licensing of individuals will consist of making checks with the Criminal Records Bureau. Most applicants will be subject to the standard disclosure level which, *inter alia*, is designed for persons applying for positions of trust, which will include security operatives. A certificate issued under this scheme contains details of all convictions on record, both spent and unspent, together with any cautions, reprimands or warnings. Standard disclosure also includes other information which is contained in government records relating to persons considered unsuitable for work with children or vulnerable adults, regardless of whether they have a criminal record.[20]

Section 21, however, makes provision for enhanced criminal record certificates to be available in respect of door supervisors for public houses and clubs and comparable venues. As mentioned earlier in this commentary, such operatives are among those who are subject to additional controls under Part 2 of Sched 2 under the Act. Section 21 enables this information to be accessible by inserting a new para (ga) under s 115(5) of the Police Act 1997. Enhanced criminal record certificates include the information obtainable under standard disclosure, but with any intelligence held on local police records.[21]

Section 22: False information

It will be a criminal offence for a person to knowingly or recklessly make any false statement to the Authority in respect of any purposes connected with its functions. This offence will be triable summarily only and punishable by a maximum of six months' imprisonment and/or a fine not exceeding level 5 on the standard scale (currently £5,000). Individual as well as corporate criminal liability will be applicable in appropriate cases under s 23, and it should be mentioned that all the new offences created under the Act will also be subject to the general criminal law regarding inchoate offences, participation and general defences.

SUPPLEMENTAL

Section 23: Criminal liability of directors etc

This section has been mentioned several times in this commentary, as it applies to all the new offences created under the Act. Section 23 provides that where an offence under any provision of the Act is committed by a body corporate with the consent, connivance or neglect on the part of a director, manager, secretary or similar officer, that person shall also be liable to prosecution.

Sections 24, 25 and 26

These sections cover the usual matters that round off a regulatory Act of this nature. Section 24 describes the manner in which the regulations under the Act are to be created, s 25 interprets certain key words and phrases in the Act such as 'premises' and 'surveillance', and s 26 contains the short title, commencement and extent of the Act. Schedules 1 and 2 were described earlier in this commentary under ss 1 and 3.

---

20 Hasan, I and Simpkins, P (2001) *Solicitors Journal*, 8 June.
21 *Ibid*.

CONCLUSION

Few would argue against the regulation of the private security industry, which is generally believed to be long overdue. It was mentioned in the introduction that the role of this expanding industry is one of increasing importance, especially in view of the expansion of public protection duties which some of the leading security companies now perform. The private security industry will almost certainly be presented with even greater challenges and responsibilities in the future; therefore, regulation will be more important than ever.

Perhaps a fitting end to this commentary would be to quote passages from the speech made by Bruce George MP during the Third Reading of the Bill. Several useful and interesting points were made during this speech by one who has persistently supported the regulation of an industry which has gathered momentum at a tremendous rate in recent years. Towards the close of the proceedings he said:

> ... I am very happy because, at long last, the private security industry is about to be regulated. Those in the industry will be the winners. They have not always realised that regulation would make them winners, but it will because it will give them something that they have been denied by their own indifference and hostility to regulation over the years. The Bill will give the industry a reputation that it can be proud of. Its previous bad reputation was deserved, because many of its members did not meet the standards set in countries such as the Netherlands, Denmark and Sweden, which have eagerly embraced regulation. International companies operating in a regulated environment elsewhere encountered no problems, and I feel rather sorry about their experience in this country, where the prevailing standards are depressing. Here, an absence of training is the norm, and the public's attitude to the security industry is a combination of mirth, hostility and indifference. That will change, and not only as a result of this long-overdue legislation. The market has changed, technology has moved forward and crime levels have risen. The police realise that they must work with technology produced in the private sector and with an industry to which they can relate. In the past, the police were the professionals and the private security industry, in some sectors, was anti-professional.[22]

He later went on to say that the Bill constituted the beginning of 'a rolling programme of improvement'[23] for the private security industry.

Many will be watching the progress of the Act now that it has begun to come into force. Without doubt, the times ahead promise to be both challenging and controversial. It will be particularly interesting to see how this statute relates to the provisions of the Police Reform Act 2002, discussed in Part II of this book. Meanwhile, issues concerned with law and order, and the administration of justice, are currently before Parliament under the Criminal Justice Bill and the Courts Bill. Whilst this book was being completed (for the time being at least), both these Bills were entering their respective committee stages. This will lead to more reforms in the near future, causing a greater burden for those who are

---

22 *Hansard*, House of Commons, Official Report, Parliamentary Debates, 8 May 2001, Cols 83–84.
23 *Ibid*, Col 85.

already struggling to keep the criminal justice system working. One hopes for a positive outcome from all these changes in return for the effort made to keep up with them.

Author's note

This commentary on the Private Security Industry Act 2001 has been largely taken from the author's article which was originally published in Justice of the Peace (Vol 166(4), 26 January 2002, pp 60–67 and Vol 166(7) 16 February 2002, pp 123–27). Our thanks go to Butterworths for their kind permission to reproduce much of this article in this book.

APPENDIX 1

POWERS OF ARREST UNDER SECTIONS 24, 116 AND SCHEDULES 1A AND 5 OF THE POLICE AND CRIMINAL EVIDENCE ACT 1984

ALL CITIZENS

MAY ARREST ANYONE:

Suspect caught *in* the act

Actually committing an arrestable offence or there are reasonable grounds for suspecting to be committing an arrestable offence.

OR

Suspect caught *after* the act

Anyone who is guilty of having committed an arrestable offence or there are reasonable grounds for suspecting this.

Suspect caught *before* the act

No power for an ordinary citizen to arrest under PACE although s 3 of the Criminal Law Act 1967 gives both citizens and the police power to use reasonable force to prevent crime, etc.

→ These conditions apply also to the police

POLICE ONLY

These conditions apply also to the police.

Or only reasonable grounds to suspect that an arrestable offence has been committed in the first place.

May arrest anyone about to commit an arrestable offence or has reasonable grounds for suspecting they are about to do so.

ARRESTABLE OFFENCES (S 24 & SCHEDULE 1A OF PACE)

Offences where sentence fixed by law, offences where a person 21 years or over (due to be reduced to 18) may be given a five year term of imprisonment on a first conviction, offences under the Customs & Excise Acts, the Official Secrets Acts of 1920 & 1989, s 1(1) of the Prevention of Crime Act 1953 (carrying offensive weapons), s 22 or 23 of the Sexual Offences Act 1956 (causing prostitution of women & procuration of a girl under 21), s 2 of the Obscene Publications Act 1959 (publication of obscene matter), s 12(1) or 25(1) of the Theft Act 1968 (taking a motor vehicle without consent & going equipped for stealing), s 3 of the Theft Act 1978 (making off without payment), s 1 of the Protection of Children Act 1978 (indecent photographs/pseudo-photographs of children), s 1(1) or (2) or 6, 1(5), 9 or 13(1)(a) or (2) or 14 of the Wildlife & Countryside Act 1981 (various offences regarding wild birds, wild animals and plants), s 39(1) of the Civil Aviation Act 1982 (trespass on aerodrome), s 21C(1) or 21D(1) of the Aviation Security Act 1982 (unauthorised presence in a restricted zone or aircraft), s 1 of the Sexual Offences Act 1985 (kerb-crawling), s 19 of the Public Order Act 1986 (publishing etc material likely to stir up racial or religious hatred), s 139(1), 139A(1) or (2) of the Criminal Justice Act 1988 (offensive weapons, knives etc in schools), s 103(1)(b) or 170(4) of the Road Traffic Act 1988 (driving whilst disqualified & failing to stop/report a personal injury road traffic accident), s 14J or 21C of the Football Spectators Act 1989 (contravention of banning order or notice), the Football (Offences) Act 1991 (pitch-invasion, indecent or racialist chanting, throwing missiles), s 60AA(7), 166 or 167 of the Criminal Justice & Public Order Act 1994 (failure to remove disguise, ticket & taxi touting), s 89(1) of the Police Act 1996 (assault on police), s 2 of the Protection from Harassment Act 1997 (harassment), s 32(1)(a) of the Crime & Disorder Act 1998 (racially or religiously aggravated harassment), s 12(4) or 46 of the Criminal Justice & Police Act 2001 (failure to surrender alcohol & placing advertisements for prostitution). Also conspiring, inciting, aiding, abetting, counselling or procuring any of the above, including attempting, except those which are triable summarily only.

Can be transformed into serious arrestable offences under s 116 if: serious harm to state security or public order, death or serious injury to any person, serious interference with the administration of justice, or substantial financial gain or loss.

CRIMES WHICH ARE ALWAYS SERIOUS ARRESTABLE OFFENCES (S 116 AND SCHEDULE 5)

Treason, murder, manslaughter, rape, kidnapping, incest with girl under the age of 13, buggery with person under the age of 16, indecent assault constituting gross indecency, drug trafficking and money laundering offences, s 170 of the Customs & Excise Management Act 1979 (importing indecent or obscene articles), s 2 of the Explosive Substances Act 1883 (causing explosion likely to endanger life or property), s 5 of the Sexual Offences Act 1956 (intercourse with girl under the age of 13), ss 16, 17 & 18 of the Firearms Act 1968 (possession of firearms with intent to injure, use of firearms or imitation firearms to resist arrest, & carrying firearms with criminal intent), s 1 of the Taking of Hostages Act 1982 (hostage-taking), s 1 of the Aviation Security Act 1982 (hijacking), s 134 of the Criminal Justice Act 1988 (torture), ss 1 & 3A of the Road Traffic Act 1988 (causing death by dangerous driving & causing death by careless driving when under the influence of drink or drugs), ss 1, 9 & 10 of the Aviation & Maritime Security Act 1990 (endangering safety at aerodromes, hijacking of ships & seizing or exercising control of fixed platforms), Arts 4 & 5 of the Channel Tunnel (Security) Order 1994 (hijacking Channel Tunnel trains & seizing or exercising control of the tunnel system), s 1 of the Protection of Children Act 1978 (indecent photographs & pseudo-photographs of children), s 2 of the Obscene Publications Act 1959 (publication of obscene matter).

APPENDIX 2

POLICE POWERS OF ARREST UNDER SECTION 25 OF THE POLICE AND CRIMINAL EVIDENCE ACT 1984

25 General arrest conditions

(1) Where a constable has reasonable grounds for suspecting that any offence which is not an arrestable offence has been committed or attempted, or is being committed or attempted, he may arrest the relevant person if it appears to him that service of a summons is impracticable or inappropriate because any of the general arrest conditions is satisfied.

(2) In this section 'the relevant person' means any person whom the constable has reasonable grounds to suspect of having committed or having attempted to commit the offence of or being in the course of committing or attempting to commit it.

(3) The general arrest conditions are –

  (a) that the name of the relevant person is unknown to, and cannot be readily ascertained by, the constable;

  (b) that the constable has reasonable grounds for doubting whether a name furnished by the relevant person as his name is his real name;

  (c) that –

    (i) the relevant person has failed to furnish a satisfactory address for service; or

    (ii) the constable has reasonable grounds for doubting whether an address furnished by the relevant person is a satisfactory address for service;

  (d) that the constable has reasonable grounds for believing that arrest is necessary to prevent the relevant person –

    (i)   causing physical injury to himself or any other person;

    (ii) suffering physical injury;

    (iii) causing loss of or damage to property;

    (iv) committing an offence against public decency; or

    (v)   causing an unlawful obstruction of the highway;

  (e) that the constable has reasonable grounds for believing that arrest is necessary to protect a child or other vulnerable person from the relevant person.

(4) For the purposes of subsection (3) above an address is a satisfactory address for service if it appears to the constable –

  (a) that the relevant person will be at it for a sufficiently long period for it to be possible to serve him with a summons; or

  (b) that some other person specified by the relevant person will accept service of a summons for the relevant person at it.

(5) Nothing in subsection (3)(d) above authorises the arrest of a person under sub-paragraph (iv) of that paragraph except where members of the public going about their normal business cannot reasonably be expected to avoid the person to be arrested.

(6) This section shall not prejudice any power of arrest conferred apart from this section.

APPENDIX 3

EXAMPLES OF 'ANY PERSON' ARREST POWERS

Section 3(4) of the Theft Act 1978[1]

Making off without payment.

Section 25(1) of the Theft Act 1968[2]

Going equipped for stealing etc.

Section 91 of the Criminal Justice Act 1967

Arrest of a person who is drunk and disorderly in a public place.

Section 41 of the Sexual Offences Act 1956

Arrest of a man soliciting or importuning for an immoral purpose in a public place.

Section 6 of the Vagrancy Act 1824

> It shall be lawful for any person whatsoever to apprehend any person who shall be found offending against this Act, and forthwith to take and convey him or her before some justice of the peace, to be dealt with in such manner as is hereinbefore directed, or to deliver him or her to any constable or other peace officer of the place where he or she should have been apprehended, to be so taken and conveyed as aforesaid …

Other examples of 'any person' arrest powers can be found under s 1 of the Licensing Act 1902 and s 11 of the Prevention of Offences Act 1851.

---

1   This offence was made an arrestable offence under Sched 1A of the Police and Criminal Evidence Act 1984 by virtue of s 48 of the Police Reform Act 2002.
2   This offence is also an arrestable offence under Sched 1A of the Police and Criminal Evidence Act 1984.

APPENDIX 4

THE TEXT OF PART 4, CHAPTER 1 AND SCHEDULES 4 AND 5 OF THE POLICE REFORM ACT 2002

PART 4

POLICE POWERS ETC

CHAPTER 1

EXERCISE OF POLICE POWERS ETC BY CIVILIANS

38 Police powers for police authority employees

(1) The chief officer of police of any police force may designate any person who–

    (a) is employed by the police authority maintaining that force, and

    (b) is under the direction and control of that chief officer,

as an officer of one or more of the descriptions specified in subsection (2).

(2) The description of officers are as follows–

    (a) community support officer;

    (b) investigating officer;

    (c) detention officer;

    (d) escort officer.

(3) A Director General may designate any person who–

    (a) is an employee of his Service Authority, and

    (b) is under the direction and control of that Director General,

as an investigating officer.

(4) A chief officer of police or a Director General shall not designate a person under this section unless he is satisfied that that person–

    (a) is a suitable person to carry out the functions for the purposes of which he is designated;

    (b) is capable of effectively carrying out those functions; and

    (c) has received adequate training in the carrying out of those functions and in the exercise and performance of the powers and duties to be conferred on him by virtue of the designation.

(5) A person designated under this section shall have the powers and duties conferred or imposed on him by the designation.

(6) Powers and duties may be conferred or imposed on a designated person by means only of the application to him by his designation of provisions of the applicable Part of Schedule 4 that are to apply to the designated person; and for this purpose the applicable Part of that Schedule is–

    (a) in the case of a person designated as a community support officer, Part 1;

    (b) in the case of a person designated as an investigating officer, Part 2;

    (c) in the case of a person designated as a detention officer, Part 3; and

    (d) in the case of a person designated as an escort officer, Part 4.

(7) An employee of a police authority or of a Service Authority authorised or required to do anything by virtue of a designation under this section–

(a) shall not be authorised or required by virtue of that designation to engage in any conduct otherwise than in the course of that employment; and

(b) shall be so authorised or required subject to such restrictions and conditions (if any) as may be specified in his designation.

(8) Where any power exercisable by any person in reliance on his designation under this section is a power which, in the case of its exercise by a constable, includes or is supplemented by a power to use reasonable force, any person exercising that power in reliance on that designation shall have the same entitlement as a constable to use reasonable force.

(9) Where any power exercisable by any person in reliance on his designation under this section includes power to use force to enter any premises, that power shall not be exercisable by that person except–

(a) in the company, and under the supervision, of a constable; or

(b) for the purpose of saving life or limb or preventing serious damage to property.

39 Police powers for contracted-out staff

(1) This section applies if a police authority has entered into a contract with a person ('the contractor') for the provision of services relating to the detention or escort of persons who have been arrested or are otherwise in custody.

(2) The chief officer of police of the police force maintained by that police authority may designate any person who is an employee of the contractor as either or both of the following–

(a) a detention officer; or

(b) an escort officer.

(3) A person designated under this section shall have the powers and duties conferred or imposed on him by the designation.

(4) A chief officer of police shall not designate a person under this section unless he is satisfied that that person–

(a) is a suitable person to carry out the functions for the purposes of which he is designated;

(b) is capable of effectively carrying out those functions; and

(c) has received adequate training in the carrying out of those functions and in the exercise and performance of the powers and duties to be conferred on him by virtue of the designation.

(5) A chief officer of police shall not designate a person under this section unless he is satisfied that the contractor is a fit and proper person to supervise the carrying out of the functions for the purposes of which that person is designated.

(6) Powers and duties may be conferred or imposed on a designated person by means only of the application to him by his designation of provisions of the applicable Part of Schedule 4 that are to apply to the designated person; and for this purpose the applicable Part of that Schedule is–

(a) in the case of a person designated as a detention officer, Part 3; and

(b) in the case of a person designated as an escort officer, Part 4.

(7) An employee of the contractor authorised or required to do anything by virtue of a designation under this section–

(a) shall not be authorised or required by virtue of that designation to engage in any conduct otherwise than in the course of that employment; and

(b) shall be so authorised or required subject to such restrictions and conditions (if any) as may be specified in his designation.

(8) Where any power exercisable by any person in reliance on his designation under this section is a power which, in the case of its exercise by a constable, includes or is supplemented by a power to use reasonable force, any person exercising that power in reliance on that designation shall have the same entitlement as a constable to use reasonable force.

(9) The Secretary of State may by regulations make provision for the handling of complaints relating to, or other instances of misconduct involving, the carrying out by any person designated under this section of the functions for the purposes of which any power or duty is conferred or imposed by his designation.

(10) Regulations under subsection (9) may, in particular, provide that any provision made by Part 2 of this Act with respect to complaints against persons serving with the police is to apply, with such modifications as may be prescribed by them, with respect to complaints against persons designated under this section.

(11) Before making regulations under this section, the Secretary of State shall consult with–

(a) persons whom he considers to represent the interests of police authorities;

(b) persons whom he considers to represent the interests of chief officers of police;

(c) the Independent Police Complaints Commission; and

(d) such other persons as he thinks fit.

(12) A designation under this section, unless it is previously withdrawn or ceases to have effect in accordance with subsection (13), shall remain in force for such period as may be specified in the designation; but it may be renewed at any time with effect from the time when it would otherwise expire.

(13) A designation under this section shall cease to have effect–

(a) if the designated person ceases to be an employee of the contractor; or

(b) if the contract between the police authority and the contractor is terminated or expires.

40 Community safety accreditation schemes

(1) The chief officer of police of any police force may, if he considers that it is appropriate to do so for the purposes specified in subsection (3), establish and maintain a scheme ('a community safety accreditation scheme').

(2) A community safety accreditation scheme is a scheme for the exercise in the chief officer's police area by persons accredited by him under section 41 of the powers conferred by their accreditations under that section.

(3) Those purposes are–

(a) contributing to community safety and security; and

(b) in co-operation with the police force for the area, combatting crime and disorder, public nuisance and other forms of anti-social behaviour.

(4) Before establishing a community safety accreditation scheme for his police area, a chief officer of any police force (other than the Commissioner of Police of the Metropolis) must consult with–

(a) the police authority maintaining that force; and

(b) every local authority any part of whose area lies within the police area.

(5) Before establishing a community safety accreditation scheme for the metropolitan police district, the Commissioner of Police of the Metropolis must consult with–

(a) the Metropolitan Police Authority;

(b) the Mayor of London; and

(c) every local authority any part of whose area lies within the metropolitan police district.

(6) In subsections (4)(b) and (5)(c) 'local authority' means–

(a) in relation to England, a district council, a London borough council, the Common Council of the City of London or the Council of the Isles of Scilly; and

(b) in relation to Wales, a county council or a county borough council.

(7) Every police plan under section 8 of the 1996 Act which is issued after the commencement of this section, and every draft of such a plan which is submitted by a chief officer of police to a police authority after the commencement of this section, must set out–

(a) whether a community safety accreditation scheme is maintained for the police area in question;

(b) if not, whether there is any proposal to establish such a scheme for that area during the period to which the plan relates;

(c) particulars of any such proposal or of any proposal to modify during that period any community safety accreditation scheme that is already maintained for that area;

(d) the extent (if any) of any arrangements for provisions specified in Schedule 4 to be applied to designated persons employed by the police authority; and

(e) the respects in which any community safety accreditation scheme that is maintained or proposed will be supplementing those arrangements during the period to which the plan relates.

(8) A community safety accreditation scheme must contain provision for the making of arrangements with employers who–

(a) are carrying on business in the police area in question, or

(b) are carrying on business in relation to the whole or any part of that area or in relation to places situated within it,

for those employers to supervise the carrying out by their employees of the community safety functions for the purposes of which powers are conferred on those employees by means of accreditations under section 41.

(9) It shall be the duty of a chief officer of police who establishes and maintains a community safety accreditation scheme to ensure that the employers of the persons on whom powers are conferred by the grant of accreditations under section 41 have established and maintain satisfactory arrangements for handling complaints relating to the carrying out by those persons of the functions for the purposes of which the powers are conferred.

41 Accreditation under community safety accreditation schemes

(1) This section applies where a chief officer of police has, for the purposes of a community safety accreditation scheme, entered into any arrangements with any employer for or with respect to the carrying out of community safety functions by employees of that employer.

(2) The chief officer of police may, on the making of an application for the purpose by such person and in such manner as he may require, grant accreditation under this section to any employee of the employer.

(3) Schedule 5 (which sets out the powers that may be conferred on accredited persons) shall have effect.

(4) A chief officer of police shall not grant accreditation to a person under this section unless he is satisfied–

(a) that that person's employer is a fit and proper person to supervise the carrying out of the functions for the purposes of which the accreditation is to be granted;

(b) that the person himself is a suitable person to exercise the powers that will be conferred on him by virtue of the accreditation;

(c) that that person is capable of effectively carrying out the functions for the purposes of which those powers are to be conferred on him; and

(d) that that person has received adequate training for the exercise of those powers.

(5) A chief officer of police may charge such fee as he considers appropriate for one or both of the following–

(a) considering an application for or for the renewal of an accreditation under this section;

(b) granting such an accreditation.

(6) A person authorised or required to do anything by virtue of an accreditation under this section–

(a) shall not be authorised or required by virtue of that accreditation to engage in any conduct otherwise than in the course of his employment by the employer with whom the chief officer of police has entered into the arrangements mentioned in subsection (1); and

(b) shall be so authorised or required subject to such other restrictions and conditions (if any) as may be specified in his accreditation.

(7) An accreditation under this section, unless it is previously withdrawn or ceases to have effect in accordance with subsection (8), shall remain in force for such period as may be specified in the accreditation; but it may be renewed at any time with effect from the time when it would otherwise expire.

(8) An accreditation under this section shall cease to have effect–

(a) if the accredited person ceases to be an employee of the person with whom the chief officer of police has entered into the arrangements mentioned in subsection (1); or

(b) if those arrangements are terminated or expire.

42 Supplementary provisions relating to designations and accreditations

(1) A person who exercises or performs any power or duty in relation to any person in reliance on his designation under section 38 or 39 or his accreditation under section 41, or who purports to do so, shall produce that designation or accreditation to that person, if requested to do so.

(2) A power exercisable by any person in reliance on his designation by a chief officer of police under section 38 or 39 or his accreditation under section 41 shall be exercisable only by a person wearing such uniform as may be–

(a) determined or approved for the purposes of this Chapter by the chief officer of police who granted the designation or accreditation; and

(b) identified or described in the designation or accreditation;

and, in the case of an accredited person, such a power shall be exercisable only if he is also wearing such badge as may be specified for the purposes of this subsection by the Secretary of State, and is wearing it in such manner, or in such place, as may be so specified.

(3) A chief officer of police who has granted a designation or accreditation to any person under section 38, 39 or 41 may at any time, by notice to the designated or accredited person, modify or withdraw that designation or accreditation.

(4) A Director General may at any time, by notice to a person he has designated as an investigating officer under section 38, modify or withdraw that designation.

(5) Where any person's designation under section 39 is modified or withdrawn, the chief officer giving notice of the modification or withdrawal shall send a copy of the notice to the contractor responsible for supervising that person in the carrying out of the functions for the purposes of which the designation was granted.

(6) Where any person's accreditation under section 41 is modified or withdrawn, the chief officer giving notice of the modification or withdrawal shall send a copy of the notice to the employer responsible for supervising that person in the carrying out of the functions for the purposes of which the accreditation was granted.

(7) For the purposes of determining liability for the unlawful conduct of employees of a police authority, conduct by such an employee in reliance or purported reliance on a designation under section 38 shall be taken to be conduct in the course of his employment by the police authority; and, in the case of a tort, that authority shall fall to be treated as a joint tortfeasor accordingly.

(8) For the purposes of determining liability for the unlawful conduct of employees of a Service Authority, conduct by such an employee in reliance or purported reliance on a designation under section 38 shall be taken to be conduct in the course of his employment; and, in the case of a tort, the Service Authority shall fall to be treated as a joint tortfeasor accordingly.

(9) For the purposes of determining liability for the unlawful conduct of employees of a contractor (within the meaning of section 39), conduct by such an employee in reliance or purported reliance on a designation under that section shall be taken to be conduct in the course of his employment by that contractor; and, in the case of a tort, that contractor shall fall to be treated as a joint tortfeasor accordingly.

(10) For the purposes of determining liability for the unlawful conduct of employees of a person with whom a chief officer of police has entered into any arrangements for the purposes of a community safety accreditation scheme, conduct by such an employee in reliance or purported reliance on an accreditation under section 41 shall be taken to be conduct in the course of his employment by that employer; and, in the case of a tort, that employer shall fall to be treated as a joint tortfeasor accordingly.

43 Railway safety accreditation scheme

(1) The Secretary of State may make regulations for the purpose of enabling the chief constable of the British Transport Police Force to establish and maintain a scheme ('a railway safety accreditation scheme').

(2) A railway safety accreditation scheme is a scheme for the exercise in, on or in the vicinity of policed premises in England and Wales, by persons accredited by the chief constable of the British Transport Police Force under the scheme, of the powers conferred on those persons by their accreditation under that scheme.

(3) The regulations may make provision–

    (a) as to the purposes for which a railway safety accreditation scheme may be established;

    (b) as to the procedure to be followed in the establishment of such a scheme; and

    (c) as to matters for which such a scheme must contain provision.

(4) The regulations may make provision as to the descriptions of persons who may be accredited under a railway safety accreditation scheme and as to the procedure and criteria to be applied for the grant of any accreditation under such a scheme.

(5) The regulations may make provision as to the powers which may be conferred on a person by an accreditation under such a scheme.

(6) Subject to subsection (7), no regulations made by virtue of subsection (5) shall permit a power to be conferred on a person accredited under a railway safety accreditation scheme which could not be conferred on an accredited person under a community safety accreditation scheme.

(7) The regulations may provide that the powers which may be conferred on a person by an accreditation under a railway safety accreditation scheme include the powers of a constable in uniform and of an authorised constable to give a penalty notice under Chapter 1 of Part 1 of the Criminal Justice and Police Act 2001 (fixed penalty notices) in respect of the following offences–

    (a) an offence under section 55 of the British Transport Commission Act 1949 (c xxix) (trespassing on a railway);

    (b) an offence under section 56 of that Act (throwing stones etc at trains or other things on railways).

(8) In relation to a person accredited under a railway safety accreditation scheme, the regulations may apply, with such modifications as may be prescribed by them, any provision of this Chapter which applies in relation to an accredited person.

(9) Before making regulations under this section the Secretary of State shall consult with–

    (a) persons whom he considers to represent the interests of chief officers of police;

    (b) the chief constable of the British Transport Police Force;

    (c) persons whom he considers to represent the interests of police authorities;

    (d) the British Transport Police Committee;

    (e) persons whom he considers to represent the interests of local authorities;

    (f) the Mayor of London; and

    (g) such other persons as he thinks fit.

(10) In this section–

'local authorities' means district councils, London borough councils, county councils in Wales, county borough councils and the Common Council of the City of London; and

'policed premises' has the meaning given by section 53(3) of the British Transport Commission Act 1949.

44 Removal of restriction on powers conferred on traffic wardens

(1) Section 96 of the Road Traffic Regulation Act 1984 (c 27) (additional powers of traffic wardens) shall be amended as follows.

(2) In subsection (2)(c) (powers under the Road Traffic Act 1988 (c 52) which may be conferred on traffic wardens), after sub-paragraph (i) there shall be inserted–

'(ia) section 67(3) (which relates to the power of a constable in uniform to stop vehicles for testing);'.

(3) In subsection (3) (traffic wardens not to be given the powers of a constable under sections 163, 164(1), (2) and (6) and 165 of the Road Traffic Act 1988 except for the purposes of exercising them in the circumstances specified in that subsection)–

(a) in the words before paragraph (a), the words '163' (which refer to the power to stop a vehicle) shall be omitted; and

(b) paragraph (c) and the word 'or' immediately preceding it shall cease to have effect.

45 Code of practice relating to chief officers' powers under Chapter 1

(1) The Secretary of State shall issue a code of practice about the exercise and performance by chief officers of police and by Directors General of their powers and duties under this Chapter.

(2) The Secretary of State may from time to time revise the whole or any part of a code of practice issued under this section.

(3) Before issuing or revising a code of practice under this section, the Secretary of State shall consult with–

(a) the Service Authority for the National Criminal Intelligence Service;

(b) the Service Authority for the National Crime Squad;

(c) persons whom he considers to represent the interests of police authorities;

(d) the Director General of the National Criminal Intelligence Service;

(e) the Director General of the National Crime Squad;

(f) persons whom he considers to represent the interests of chief officers of police;

(g) persons whom he considers to represent the interests of local authorities;

(h) the Mayor of London; and

(i) such other persons as he thinks fit.

(4) The Secretary of State shall lay any code of practice issued by him under this section, and any revisions of any such code, before Parliament.

(5) In discharging any function to which a code of practice under this section relates, a chief officer of police or a Director General shall have regard to the code.

(6) For the purposes of subsection (3)(g), 'local authorities' means district councils, London borough councils, county councils in Wales, county borough councils, the Common Council of the City of London and the Council of the Isles of Scilly.

46 Offences against designated and accredited persons etc

(1) Any person who assaults–

(a) a designated person in the execution of his duty;

(b) an accredited person in the execution of his duty; or

(c) a person assisting a designated or accredited person in the execution of his duty,

is guilty of an offence and shall be liable, on summary conviction, to imprisonment for a term not exceeding six months or to a fine not exceeding level 5 on the standard scale, or to both.

(2) Any person who resists or wilfully obstructs–

(a) a designated person in the execution of his duty;

(b) an accredited person in the execution of his duty; or

(c) a person assisting a designated or accredited person in the execution of his duty,

is guilty of an offence and shall be liable, on summary conviction, to imprisonment for a term not exceeding one month or to a fine not exceeding level 3 on the standard scale, or to both.

(3) Any person who, with intent to deceive–

(a) impersonates a designated person or an accredited person;

(b) makes any statement or does any act calculated falsely to suggest that he is a designated person or that he is an accredited person; or

(c) makes any statement or does any act calculated falsely to suggest that he has powers as a designated or accredited person that exceed the powers he actually has,

is guilty of an offence and shall be liable, on summary conviction, to imprisonment for a term not exceeding six months or to a fine not exceeding level 5 on the standard scale, or to both.

(4) In this section references to the execution by a designated person or accredited person of his duty are references to his exercising any power or performing any duty which is his by virtue of his designation or accreditation.

47 Interpretation of Chapter 1

(1) In this Chapter–

'accredited person' means a person in relation to whom an accreditation under section 41 is for the time being in force;

'community safety functions' means any functions the carrying out of which would be facilitated by the ability to exercise one or more of the powers mentioned in Schedule 5;

'conduct' includes omissions and statements;

'designated person' means a person in relation to whom a designation under section 38 or 39 is for the time being in force;

'Director General' means–

(a) the Director General of the National Criminal Intelligence Service; or

(b) the Director General of the National Crime Squad.

'Service Authority' means–

(a) in relation to employment with the National Criminal Intelligence Service or to its Director General, the Service Authority for the National Criminal Intelligence Service; and

(b) in relation to employment with the National Crime Squad or to its Director General, the Service Authority for the National Crime Squad.

(2) In this Chapter–

   (a) references to carrying on business include references to carrying out functions under any enactment; and

   (b) references to the employees of a person carrying on business include references to persons holding office under a person, and references to employers shall be construed accordingly.

SCHEDULE 4
POWERS EXERCISABLE BY POLICE CIVILIANS
PART 1
COMMUNITY SUPPORT OFFICERS

Powers to issue fixed penalty notices

1(1) Where a designation applies this paragraph to any person, that person shall have the powers specified in sub-paragraph (2) in relation to any individual who he has reason to believe has committed a relevant fixed penalty offence at a place within the relevant police area.

  (2) Those powers are the following powers so far as exercisable in respect of a relevant fixed penalty offence–

   (a) the powers of a constable in uniform and of an authorised constable to give a penalty notice under Chapter 1 of Part 1 of the Criminal Justice and Police Act 2001 (c 16) (fixed penalty notices in respect of offences of disorder);

   (b) the power of a constable in uniform to give a person a fixed penalty notice under section 54 of the Road Traffic Offenders Act 1988 (c 53) (fixed penalty notices) in respect of an offence under section 72 of the Highway Act 1835 (c 50) (riding on a footway) committed by cycling;

   (c) the power of an authorised officer of a local authority to give a notice under section 4 of the Dogs (Fouling of Land) Act 1996 (c 20) (fixed penalty notices in respect of dog fouling); and

   (d) the power of an authorised officer of a litter authority to give a notice under section 88 of the Environmental Protection Act 1990 (c 43) (fixed penalty notices in respect of litter).

  (3) In this paragraph 'relevant fixed penalty offence', in relation to a designated person, means an offence which–

   (a) is an offence by reference to which a notice may be given to a person in exercise of any of the powers mentioned in sub-paragraph 1(2)(a) to (d); and

   (b) is specified or described in that person's designation as an offence he has been designated to enforce under this paragraph.

Power to detain etc

2(1) This paragraph applies if a designation applies it to any person.

  (2) Where that person has reason to believe that another person has committed a relevant offence in the relevant police area, he may require that other person to give him his name and address.

  (3) Where, in a case in which a requirement under sub-paragraph (2) has been imposed on another person–

   (a) that other person fails to comply with the requirement; or

   (b) the person who imposed the requirement has reasonable grounds for suspecting that the other person has given him a name or address that is false or inaccurate,

the person who imposed the requirement may require the other person to wait with him, for a period not exceeding thirty minutes, for the arrival of a constable.

(4) A person who has been required under sub-paragraph (3) to wait with a person to whom this Part of this Schedule applies may, if requested to do so, elect that (instead of waiting) he will accompany the person imposing the requirement to a police station in the relevant police area.

(5) A person who–

(a) fails to comply with a requirement under sub-paragraph (2);

(b) makes off while subject to a requirement under sub-paragraph (3); or

(c) makes off while accompanying a person to a police station in accordance with an election under sub-paragraph (4),

is guilty of an offence and shall be liable, on summary conviction, to a fine not exceeding level 3 on the standard scale.

(6) In this paragraph 'relevant offence', in relation to a person to whom this paragraph applies, means any offence which is–

(a) a relevant fixed penalty offence for the purposes of the application of paragraph 1 to that person; or

(b) an offence the commission of which appears to that person to have caused–

(i) injury, alarm or distress to any other person; or

(ii) the loss of, or any damage to, any other person's property;

but a designation applying this paragraph to any person may provide that an offence is not to be treated as a relevant offence by virtue of paragraph (b) unless it satisfies such other conditions as may be specified in the designation.

Power to require name and address of person acting in an anti-social manner

3(1) Where a designation applies this paragraph to any person, that person shall, in the relevant police area, have the powers of a constable in uniform under section 50 to require a person whom he has reason to believe to have been acting, or to be acting, in an anti-social manner (within the meaning of section 1 of the Crime and Disorder Act 1998 (c 37) (anti-social behaviour orders)) to give his name and address.

(2) Sub-paragraphs (3) to (5) of paragraph 2 apply in the case of a requirement imposed by virtue of sub-paragraph (1) as they apply in the case of a requirement under sub-paragraph (2) of that paragraph.

Power to use reasonable force to detain person

4(1) This paragraph applies where a designation–

(a) applies this paragraph to a person to whom any or all of paragraphs 1 to 3 are also applied; and

(b) sets out the matters in respect of which that person has the power conferred by this paragraph.

(2) The matters that may be set out in a designation as the matters in respect of which a person has the power conferred by this paragraph shall be confined to–

(a) offences that are relevant penalty notice offences for the purposes of the application of paragraph 1 to the designated person;

(b) offences that are relevant offences for the purposes of the application of paragraph 2 to the designated person; and

(c) behaviour that constitutes acting in an anti-social manner (within the meaning of section 1 of the Crime and Disorder Act 1998 (c 37) (anti-social behaviour orders)).

(3) In any case in which a person to whom this paragraph applies has imposed a requirement on any other person under paragraph 2(2) or 3(1) in respect of anything appearing to him to be a matter set out in the designation, he may use reasonable force to prevent that other person from making off while he is either–

(a) subject to a requirement imposed in that case by the designated person under sub-paragraph (3) of paragraph 2; or

(b) accompanying the designated person to a police station in accordance with an election made in that case under sub-paragraph (4) of that paragraph.

Alcohol consumption in designated public places

5   Where a designation applies this paragraph to any person, that person shall, within the relevant police area, have the powers of a constable under section 12 of the Criminal Justice and Police Act 2001 (c 16) (alcohol consumption in public places)–

(a) to impose a requirement under subsection (2) of that section; and

(b) to dispose under subsection (3) of that section of anything surrendered to him;

and that section shall have effect in relation to the exercise of those powers by that person as if the references to a constable in subsections (1) and (5) were references to that person.

Confiscation of alcohol

6   Where a designation applies this paragraph to any person, that person shall, within the relevant police area, have the powers of a constable under section 1 of the Confiscation of Alcohol (Young Persons) Act 1997 (c 33) (confiscation of intoxicating liquor)–

(a) to impose a requirement under subsection (1) of that section; and

(b) to dispose under subsection (2) of that section of anything surrendered to him;

and that section shall have effect in relation to the exercise of those powers by that person as if the references to a constable in subsections (1) and (4) (but not the reference in subsection (5) (arrest)) were references to that person.

Confiscation of tobacco etc

7   Where a designation applies this paragraph to any person, that person shall, within the relevant police area, have–

(a) the power to seize anything that a constable in uniform has a duty to seize under subsection (3) of section 7 of the Children and Young Persons Act 1933 (c 12) (seizure of tobacco etc from young persons); and

(b) the power to dispose of anything that a constable may dispose of under that subsection;

and the power to dispose of anything shall be a power to dispose of it in such manner as the police authority may direct.

Entry to save life or limb or prevent serious damage to property

8   Where a designation applies this paragraph to any person, that person shall have the powers of a constable under section 17 of the 1984 Act to enter and search any premises in the relevant police area for the purpose of saving life or limb or preventing serious damage to property.

Seizure of vehicles used to cause alarm etc

9(1) Where a designation applies this paragraph to any person–

(a) that person shall, within the relevant police area, have all the powers of a constable in uniform under section 59 of this Act which are set out in subsection (3) of that section; and

(b) references in that section to a constable, in relation to the exercise of any of those powers by that person, are references to that person.

(2) A person to whom this paragraph applies shall not enter any premises in exercise of the power conferred by section 59(3)(c) except in the company, and under the supervision, of a constable.

Abandoned vehicles

10 Where a designation applies this paragraph to any person, that person shall have any such powers in the relevant police area as are conferred on persons designated under that section by regulations under section 99 of the Road Traffic Regulation Act 1984 (c 27) (removal of abandoned vehicles).

Power to stop vehicle for testing

11 Where a designation applies this paragraph to any person, that person shall, within the relevant police area, have the power of a constable in uniform to stop a vehicle under subsection (3) of section 67 of the Road Traffic Act 1988 (c 52) for the purposes of a test under subsection (1) of that section.

Power to control traffic for purposes of escorting a load of exceptional dimensions

12(1) Where a designation applies this paragraph to any person, that person shall have, for the purpose of escorting a vehicle or trailer carrying a load of exceptional dimensions either to or from the relevant police area, the power of a constable engaged in the regulation of traffic in a road–

   (a) to direct a vehicle to stop;

   (b) to make a vehicle proceed in, or keep to, a particular line of traffic; and

   (c) to direct pedestrians to stop.

   (2) Sections 35 and 37 of the Road Traffic Act 1988 (offences of failing to comply with directions of constable engaged in regulation of traffic in a road) shall have effect in relation to the exercise of those powers for the purpose mentioned in sub-paragraph (1) by a person whose designation applies this paragraph to him as if the references to a constable engaged in regulation of traffic in a road were references to that person.

   (3) The powers conferred by virtue of this paragraph may be exercised in any police area in England and Wales.

   (4) In this paragraph 'vehicle or trailer carrying a load of exceptional dimensions' means a vehicle or trailer the use of which is authorised by an order made by the Secretary of State under section 44(1)(d) of the Road Traffic Act 1988.

Carrying out of road checks

13 Where a designation applies this paragraph to any person, that person shall have the following powers in the relevant police area–

   (a) the power to carry out any road check the carrying out of which by a police officer is authorised under section 4 of the 1984 Act (road checks); and

   (b) for the purpose of exercising that power, the power conferred by section 163 of the Road Traffic Act 1988 (c 52) (power of police to stop vehicles) on a constable in uniform to stop a vehicle.

Cordoned areas

14 Where a designation applies this paragraph to any person, that person shall, in relation to any cordoned area in the relevant police area, have all the powers of a constable in uniform under section 36 of the Terrorism Act 2000 (c 11) (enforcement of cordoned area) to give orders, make arrangements or impose prohibitions or restrictions.

Power to stop and search vehicles etc in authorised areas

15(1) Where a designation applies this paragraph to any person–

   (a) that person shall, in any authorised area within the relevant police area, have all the powers of a constable in uniform by virtue of section 44(1)(a) and (d) and (2)(b) and 45(2) of the Terrorism Act 2000 (powers of stop and search)–

      (i) to stop and search vehicles;

      (ii) to search anything in or on a vehicle or anything carried by the driver of a vehicle or any passenger in a vehicle;

      (iii) to search anything carried by a pedestrian; and

      (iv) to seize and retain any article discovered in the course of a search carried out by him or by a constable by virtue of any provision of section 44(1) or (2) of that Act;

and

(b) the references to a constable in subsections (1) and (4) of section 45 of that Act (which relate to the exercise of those powers) shall have effect in relation to the exercise of any of those powers by that person as references to that person.

(2) A person shall not exercise any power of stop, search or seizure by virtue of this paragraph except in the company, and under the supervision, of a constable.

PART 2

INVESTIGATING OFFICERS

Search warrants

16 Where a designation applies this paragraph to any person–

(a) he may apply as if he were a constable for a warrant under section 8 of the 1984 Act (warrants for entry and search) in respect of any premises in the relevant police area;

(b) the persons to whom a warrant to enter and search any such premises may be issued under that section shall include that person;

(c) that person shall have the power of a constable under section 8(2) of that Act in any premises in the relevant police area to seize and retain things for which a search has been authorised under subsection (1) of that section;

(d) section 15 of that Act (safeguards) shall have effect in relation to the issue of such a warrant to that person as it has effect in relation to the issue of a warrant under section 8 of that Act to a constable;

(e) section 16 of that Act (execution of warrants) shall have effect in relation to any warrant to enter and search premises that is issued (whether to that person or to any other person) in respect of premises in the relevant police area as if references in that section to a constable included references to that person;

(f) section 19(6) of that Act (protection for legally privileged material from seizure) shall have effect in relation to the seizure of anything by that person by virtue of sub-paragraph (c) as it has effect in relation to the seizure of anything by a constable;

(g) section 20 of that Act (extension of powers of seizure to computerised information) shall have effect in relation to the power of seizure conferred on that person by virtue of sub-paragraph (c) as it applies in relation to the power of seizure conferred on a constable by section 8(2) of that Act;

(h) section 21(1) and (2) of that Act (provision of record of seizure) shall have effect in relation to the seizure of anything by that person in exercise of the power conferred on him by virtue of sub-paragraph (c) as if the references to a constable and to an officer included references to that person; and

(i) sections 21(3) to (8) and 22 of that Act (access, copying and retention) shall have effect in relation to anything seized by that person in exercise of that power, or taken away by him following the imposition of a requirement by virtue of sub-paragraph (g)–

      (i) as they have effect in relation to anything seized in exercise of the power conferred on a constable by section 8(2) of that Act or taken away by a constable following the imposition of a requirement by virtue of section 20 of that Act; and

  (ii) as if the references to a constable in subsections (3), (4) and (5) of section 21 included references to a person to whom this paragraph applies.

Access to excluded and special procedure material

17 Where a designation applies this paragraph to any person–

 (a) he shall have the powers of a constable under section 9(1) of the 1984 Act (special provisions for access) to obtain access, in accordance with Schedule 1 to that Act and the following provisions of this paragraph, to excluded material and special procedure material;

 (b) that Schedule shall have effect for the purpose of conferring those powers on that person as if–

  (i) the references in paragraphs 1, 4, 5, 12 and 13 of that Schedule to a constable were references to that person; and

  (ii) the references in paragraphs 12 and 14 of that Schedule to premises were references to premises in the relevant police area;

 (c) section 19(6) of that Act (protection for legally privileged material from seizure) shall have effect in relation to the seizure of anything by that person in exercise of the power conferred on him by paragraph 13 of Schedule 1 to that Act as it has effect in relation to the seizure of anything under that paragraph by a constable;

 (d) section 20 of that Act (extension of powers of seizure to computerised information) shall have effect in relation the power of seizure conferred on that person by paragraph 13 of Schedule 1 to that Act as it applies in relation to the power of seizure conferred on a constable by that paragraph;

 (e) section 21(1) and (2) of that Act (provision of record of seizure) shall have effect in relation to the seizure of anything by that person in exercise of the power conferred on him by paragraph 13 of Schedule 1 to that Act as if the references to a constable and to an officer included references to that person; and

 (f) sections 21(3) to (8) and 22 of that Act (access, copying and retention) shall have effect in relation to anything seized by that person in exercise of that power or taken away by him following the imposition of a requirement by virtue of sub-paragraph (d), and to anything produced to him under paragraph 4(a) of Schedule 1 to that Act–

  (i) as they have effect in relation to anything seized in exercise of the power conferred on a constable by paragraph 13 of that Schedule or taken away by a constable following the imposition of a requirement by virtue of section 20 of that Act or, as the case may be, to anything produced to a constable under paragraph 4(a) of that Schedule; and

  (ii) as if the references to a constable in subsections (3), (4) and (5) of section 21 included references to a person to whom this paragraph applies.

Entry and search after arrest

18 Where a designation applies this paragraph to any person–

 (a) he shall have the powers of a constable under section 18 of the 1984 Act (entry and search after arrest) to enter and search any premises in the relevant police area and to seize and retain anything for which he may search under that section;

 (b) subsections (5) and (6) of that section (power to carry out search before arrested person taken to police station and duty to inform senior officer) shall have effect in relation to any exercise by that person of those powers as if the references in those subsections to a constable were references to that person;

 (c) section 19(6) of that Act (protection for legally privileged material from seizure) shall have effect in relation to the seizure of anything by that person by virtue of sub-paragraph (a) as it has effect in relation to the seizure of anything by a constable;

(d) section 20 of that Act (extension of powers of seizure to computerised information) shall have effect in relation to the power of seizure conferred on that person by virtue of sub-paragraph (a) as it applies in relation to the power of seizure conferred on a constable by section 18(2) of that Act;

(e) section 21(1) and (2) of that Act (provision of record of seizure) shall have effect in relation to the seizure of anything by that person in exercise of the power conferred on him by virtue of sub-paragraph (a) as if the references to a constable and to an officer included references to that person; and

(f) sections 21(3) to (8) and 22 of that Act (access, copying and retention) shall have effect in relation to anything seized by that person in exercise of that power or taken away by him following the imposition of a requirement by virtue of sub-paragraph (d)–

(i) as they have effect in relation to anything seized in exercise of the power conferred on a constable by section 18(2) of that Act or taken away by a constable following the imposition of a requirement by virtue of section 20 of that Act; and

(ii) as if the references to a constable in subsections (3), (4) and (5) of section 21 included references to a person to whom this paragraph applies.

General power of seizure

19 Where a designation applies this paragraph to any person–

(a) he shall, when lawfully on any premises in the relevant police area, have the same powers as a constable under section 19 of the 1984 Act (general powers of seizure) to seize things;

(b) he shall also have the powers of a constable to impose a requirement by virtue of subsection (4) of that section in relation to information accessible from such premises;

(c) subsection (6) of that section (protection for legally privileged material from seizure) shall have effect in relation to the seizure of anything by that person by virtue of sub-paragraph (a) as it has effect in relation to the seizure of anything by a constable;

(d) section 21(1) and (2) of that Act (provision of record of seizure) shall have effect in relation to the seizure of anything by that person in exercise of the power conferred on him by virtue of sub-paragraph (a) as if the references to a constable and to an officer included references to that person; and

(e) sections 21(3) to (8) and 22 of that Act (access, copying and retention) shall have effect in relation to anything seized by that person in exercise of that power or taken away by him following the imposition of a requirement by virtue of sub-paragraph (b)–

(i) as they have effect in relation to anything seized in exercise of the power conferred on a constable by section 19(2) or (3) of that Act or taken away by a constable following the imposition of a requirement by virtue of section 19(4) of that Act; and

(ii) as if the references to a constable in subsections (3), (4) and (5) of section 21 included references to a person to whom this paragraph applies.

Access and copying in the case of things seized by constables

20 Where a designation applies this paragraph to any person, section 21 of the 1984 Act (access and copying) shall have effect in relation to anything seized in the relevant police area by a constable as if the references to a constable in subsections (3), (4) and (5) of section 21 (supervision of access and photographing of seized items) included references to a person to whom this paragraph applies.

Arrest at a police station for another offence

21(1) Where a designation applies this paragraph to any person, he shall have the power to make an arrest at any police station in the relevant police area in any case where an arrest–

(a) is required to be made under section 31 of the 1984 Act (arrest for a further offence of a person already at a police station); or

(b) would be so required if the reference in that section to a constable included a reference to a person to whom this paragraph applies.

(2) Section 36 of the Criminal Justice and Public Order Act 1994 (c 33) (consequences of failure by arrested person to account for objects etc) shall apply (without prejudice to the effect of any designation applying paragraph 23) in the case of a person arrested in exercise of the power exercisable by virtue of this paragraph as it applies in the case of a person arrested by a constable.

Power to transfer persons into custody of investigating officers

22(1) Where a designation applies this paragraph to any person, the custody officer for a designated police station in the relevant police area may transfer or permit the transfer to him of a person in police detention for an offence which is being investigated by the person to whom this paragraph applies.

(2) A person into whose custody another person is transferred under sub-paragraph (1)–

(a) shall be treated for all purposes as having that person in his lawful custody;

(b) shall be under a duty to prevent his escape; and

(c) shall be entitled to use reasonable force to keep that person in his custody.

(3) Where a person is transferred into the custody of a person to whom this paragraph applies, in accordance with sub-paragraph (1), subsections (2) and (3) of section 39 of the 1984 Act shall have effect as if–

(a) references to the transfer of a person in police detention into the custody of a police officer investigating an offence for which that person is in police detention were references to that person's transfer into the custody of the person to whom this paragraph applies; and

(b) references to the officer to whom the transfer is made and to the officer investigating the offence were references to the person to whom this paragraph applies.

Power to require arrested person to account for certain matters

23 Where a designation applies this paragraph to any person–

(a) he shall have the powers of a constable under sections 36(1)(c) and 37(1)(c) of the Criminal Justice and Public Order Act 1994 (c 33) to request a person who–

(i) has been arrested by a constable, or by any person to whom paragraph 21 applies, and

(ii) is detained at any place in the relevant police area,

to account for the presence of an object, substance or mark or for the presence of the arrested person at a particular place; and

(b) the references to a constable in sections 36(1)(b) and (c) and (4) and 37(1)(b) and (c) and (3) of that Act shall have effect accordingly as including references to the person to whom this paragraph is applied.

Extended powers of seizure

24 Where a designation applies this paragraph to any person–

(a) the powers of a constable under Part 2 of the Criminal Justice and Police Act 2001 (c 16) (extension of powers of seizure) that are exercisable in the case of a constable by reference to a power of a constable that is conferred on that person by virtue of the provisions of this Part of this Schedule shall be exercisable by that person by reference to that power to the same extent as in the case of a constable but in relation only to premises in the relevant police area and things found on any such premises; and

(b) section 56 of that Act (retention of property seized by a constable) shall have effect as if the property referred to in subsection (1) of that section included property seized by that person at any time when he was lawfully on any premises in the relevant police area.

PART 3
DETENTION OFFICERS

Attendance at police station for fingerprinting

25 Where a designation applies this paragraph to any person, he shall, in respect of police stations in the relevant police area, have the power of a constable under section 27(1) of the 1984 Act (fingerprinting of suspects) to require a person to attend a police station in order to have his fingerprints taken.

Non-intimate searches of detained persons

26(1) Where a designation applies this paragraph to any person, he shall have the powers of a constable under section 54 of the 1984 Act (non-intimate searches of detained persons)–

   (a) to carry out a search under that section of any person at a police station in the relevant police area or of any other person otherwise in police detention in that area; and

   (b) to seize or retain, or cause to be seized or retained, anything found on such a search.

   (2) Subsections (6C) and (9) of section 54 of that Act (restrictions on power to seize personal effects and searches to be carried out by a member of the same sex) shall apply to the exercise by a person to whom this paragraph is applied of any power exercisable by virtue of this paragraph as they apply to the exercise of the power in question by a constable.

Searches and examinations to ascertain identity

27 Where a designation applies this paragraph to any person, he shall have the powers of a constable under section 54A of the 1984 Act (searches and examinations to ascertain identity)–

   (a) to carry out a search or examination at any police station in the relevant police area; and

   (b) to take a photograph at any such police station of an identifying mark.

Intimate searches of detained persons

28(1) Where a designation applies this paragraph to any person, he shall have the powers of a constable by virtue of section 55(6) of the 1984 Act (intimate searches) to carry out an intimate search of a person at any police station in the relevant police area.

   (2) Subsection (7) of section 55 of that Act (no intimate search to be carried out by a constable of the opposite sex) shall apply to the exercise by a person to whom this paragraph applies of any power exercisable by virtue of this paragraph as it applies to the exercise of the power in question by a constable.

Fingerprinting without consent

29 Where a designation applies this paragraph to any person–

   (a) he shall have, at any police station in the relevant police area, the power of a constable under section 61 of the 1984 Act (fingerprinting) to take fingerprints without the appropriate consent; and

   (b) the requirement by virtue of subsection (7A)(a) of that section that a person must be informed by an officer that his fingerprints may be the subject of a speculative search shall be capable of being discharged, in the case of a person at such a station, by his being so informed by the person to whom this paragraph applies.

Warnings about intimate samples

30 Where a designation applies this paragraph to any person, the requirement by virtue of section 62(7A)(a) of the 1984 Act (intimate samples) that a person must be informed by an officer that a sample taken from him may be the subject of a speculative search shall be capable of being discharged, in the case of a person in a police station in the relevant police area, by his being so informed by the person to whom this paragraph applies.

Non-intimate samples

31 Where a designation applies this paragraph to any person–

(a) he shall have the power of a constable under section 63 of the 1984 Act (non-intimate samples), in the case of a person in a police station in the relevant police area, to take a non-intimate sample without the appropriate consent;

(b) the requirement by virtue of subsection (6) of that section (information about authorisation) that a person must be informed by an officer of the matters mentioned in that subsection shall be capable of being discharged, in the case of an authorisation in relation to a person in a police station in the relevant police area, by his being so informed by the person to whom this paragraph applies; and

(c) the requirement by virtue of subsection (8B)(a) of that section that a person must be informed by an officer that a sample taken from him may be the subject of a speculative search shall be capable of being discharged, in the case of a person in such a police station, by his being so informed by the person to whom this paragraph applies.

Attendance at police station for the taking of a sample

32 Where a designation applies this paragraph to any person, he shall, as respects any police station in the relevant police area, have the power of a constable under subsection (4) of section 63A of the 1984 Act (supplementary provisions relating to fingerprints and samples) to require a person to attend a police station in order to have a sample taken.

Photographing persons in police detention

33 Where a designation applies this paragraph to any person, he shall, at police stations in the relevant police area, have the power of a constable under section 64A of the 1984 Act (photographing of suspects etc) to take a photograph of a person detained at a police station.

PART 4
ESCORT OFFICERS

Power to take an arrested person to a police station

34(1) Where a designation applies this paragraph to any person–

(a) the persons who, in the case of a person arrested by a constable in the relevant police area, are authorised for the purposes of subsection (1) of section 30 of the 1984 Act (procedure on arrest of person elsewhere than at a police station) to take the person arrested to a police station in that area shall include that person;

(b) that section shall have effect in relation to the exercise by that person of the power conferred by virtue of paragraph (a) as if the references to a constable in subsections (3), (4)(a) and (10) (but not the references in subsections (5) to (9)) included references to that person; and

(c) a person who is taking another person to a police station in exercise of the power conferred by virtue of paragraph (a)–

(i) shall be treated for all purposes as having that person in his lawful custody;

(ii) shall be under a duty to prevent his escape; and

(iii) shall be entitled to use reasonable force to keep that person in his charge.

(2) Without prejudice to any designation under paragraph 26, where a person has another in his lawful custody by virtue of sub-paragraph (1) of this paragraph–

(a) he shall have the same powers under subsections (6A) and (6B) of section 54 of the 1984 Act (non-intimate searches) as a constable has in the case of a person in police detention–

(i) to carry out a search of the other person; and

(ii) to seize or retain, or cause to be seized or retained, anything found on such a search;

(b) subsections (6C) and (9) of that section (restrictions on power to seize personal effects and searches to be carried out by a member of the same sex) shall apply to the exercise by a person to whom this paragraph is applied of any power exercisable by virtue of this sub-paragraph as they apply to the exercise of the power in question by a constable.

Escort of persons in police detention

35(1) Where a designation applies this paragraph to any person, that person may be authorised by the custody officer for any designated police station in the relevant police area to escort a person in police detention–

(a) from that police station to another police station in that or any other police area; or

(b) from that police station to any other place specified by the custody officer and then either back to that police station or on to another police station in that area or in another police area.

(2) Where a designation applies this paragraph to any person, that person may be authorised by the custody officer for any designated police station outside the relevant police area to escort a person in police detention–

(a) from that police station to a designated police station in that area; or

(b) from that police station to any place in that area specified by the custody officer and either back to that police station or on to another police station (whether in that area or elsewhere).

(3) A person who is escorting another in accordance with an authorisation under sub-paragraph (1) or (2)–

(a) shall be treated for all purposes as having that person in his lawful custody;

(b) shall be under a duty to prevent his escape; and

(c) shall be entitled to use reasonable force to keep that person in his charge.

(4) Without prejudice to any designation under paragraph 26, where a person has another in his lawful custody by virtue of sub-paragraph (3) of this paragraph–

(a) he shall have the same powers under subsections (6A) and (6B) of section 54 of the 1984 Act (non-intimate searches) as a constable has in the case of a person in police detention–

(i) to carry out a search of the other person; and

(ii) to seize or retain, or cause to be seized or retained, anything found on such a search;

(b) subsections (6C) and (9) of that section (restrictions on power to seize personal effects and searches to be carried out by a member of the same sex) shall apply to the exercise by a person to whom this paragraph is applied of any power exercisable by virtue of this sub-paragraph as they apply to the exercise of the power in question by a constable.

(5) Section 39(2) of that Act (responsibilities of custody officer transferred to escort) shall have effect where the custody officer for any police station transfers or permits the transfer of any person to the custody of a person who by virtue of this

paragraph has lawful custody outside the police station of the person transferred as it would apply if the person to whom this paragraph applies were a police officer.

PART 5
INTERPRETATION OF SCHEDULE

36(1) In this Schedule 'the relevant police area'–

   (a) in relation to a designation under section 38 or 39 by the chief officer of any police force, means the police area for which that force is maintained; and

   (b) in relation to a designation under section 38 by a Director General, means England and Wales.

   (2) In this Schedule 'a designation' means a designation under section 38.

   (3) In Parts 3 and 4 of this Schedule 'a designation' also includes a designation under section 39.

   (4) Expressions used in this Schedule and in the 1984 Act have the same meanings in this Schedule as in that Act.

SCHEDULE 5
POWERS EXERCISABLE BY ACCREDITED PERSONS

Power to issue fixed penalty notices

1(1) An accredited person whose accreditation specifies that this paragraph applies to him shall have the powers specified in sub-paragraph (2) in relation to any individual who he has reason to believe has committed or is committing a relevant fixed penalty offence at a place within the relevant police area.

   (2) Those powers are the following powers so far as exercisable in respect of a relevant offence–

   (a) the power of a constable in uniform to give a person a fixed penalty notice under section 54 of the Road Traffic Offenders Act 1988 (c 53) (fixed penalty notices) in respect of an offence under section 72 of the Highway Act 1835 (c 50) (riding on a footway) committed by cycling;

   (b) the power of an authorised officer of a local authority to give a notice under section 4 of the Dogs (Fouling of Land) Act 1996 (c 20) (fixed penalty notices in respect of dog fouling); and

   (c) the power of an authorised officer of a litter authority to give a notice under section 88 of the Environmental Protection Act 1990 (c 43) (fixed penalty notices in respect of litter).

   (3) In this paragraph 'relevant fixed penalty offence', in relation to an accredited person, means an offence which–

   (a) is an offence by reference to which a notice may be given to a person in exercise of any of the powers mentioned in sub-paragraph (2)(a) to (c); and

   (b) is specified or described in that person's accreditation as an offence he has been accredited to enforce.

Power to require giving of name and address

2(1) Where an accredited person whose accreditation specifies that this paragraph applies to him has reason to believe that another person has committed a relevant offence in the relevant police area, he may require that other person to give him his name and address.

   (2) A person who fails to comply with a requirement under sub-paragraph (1) is guilty of an offence and shall be liable, on summary conviction, to a fine not exceeding level 3 on the standard scale.

   (3) In this paragraph 'relevant offence', in relation to any accredited person, means any offence which is–

(a) a relevant fixed penalty offence for the purposes of any powers exercisable by the accredited person by virtue of paragraph 1; or

(b) an offence the commission of which appears to the accredited person to have caused–

   (i) injury, alarm or distress to any other person; or

   (ii) the loss of, or any damage to, any other person's property;

but the accreditation of an accredited person may provide that an offence is not to be treated as a relevant offence by virtue of paragraph (b) unless it satisfies such other conditions as may be specified in the accreditation.

Power to require name and address of person acting in an anti-social manner

3   An accredited person whose accreditation specifies that this paragraph applies to him shall, in the relevant police area, have the powers of a constable in uniform under section 50 to require a person whom he has reason to believe to have been acting, or to be acting, in an anti-social manner (within the meaning of section 1 of the Crime and Disorder Act 1998 (c 37) (anti-social behaviour orders)) to give his name and address.

Alcohol consumption in designated public places

4   An accredited person whose accreditation specifies that this paragraph applies to him shall, within the relevant police area, have the powers of a constable under section 12 of the Criminal Justice and Police Act 2001 (c 16) (alcohol consumption in public places)–

(a) to impose a requirement under subsection (2) of that section; and

(b) to dispose under subsection (3) of that section of anything surrendered to him;

and that section shall have effect in relation to the exercise of those powers by that person as if the references to a constable in subsections (1) and (5) were references to the accredited person.

Confiscation of alcohol

5   An accredited person whose accreditation specifies that this paragraph applies to him shall, within the relevant police area, have the powers of a constable under section 1 of the Confiscation of Alcohol (Young Persons) Act 1997 (c 33) (confiscation of intoxicating liquor)–

(a) to impose a requirement under subsection (1) of that section; and

(b) to dispose under subsection (2) of that section of anything surrendered to him;

and that section shall have effect in relation to the exercise of those powers by that person as if the references to a constable in subsections (1) and (4) (but not the reference in subsection (5) (arrest)) were references to the accredited person.

Confiscation of tobacco etc

6(1) An accredited person whose accreditation specifies that this paragraph applies to him shall, within the relevant police area, have–

(a) the power to seize anything that a constable in uniform has a duty to seize under subsection (3) of section 7 of the Children and Young Persons Act 1933 (c 12) (seizure of tobacco etc from young persons); and

(b) the power to dispose of anything that a constable may dispose of under that subsection;

and the power to dispose of anything shall be a power to dispose of it in such manner as the relevant employer of the accredited person may direct.

(2) In this paragraph 'relevant employer', in relation to an accredited person, means the person with whom the chief officer of police for the relevant police area has entered into arrangements under section 40.

Abandoned vehicles

7   An accredited person whose accreditation specifies that this paragraph applies to him shall have all such powers in the relevant police area as are conferred on accredited persons by regulations under section 99 of the Road Traffic Regulation Act 1984 (c 27) (removal of abandoned vehicles).

Power to stop vehicle for testing

8   A person whose accreditation specifies that this paragraph applies to him shall, within the relevant police area, have the power of a constable in uniform to stop a vehicle under subsection (3) of section 67 of the Road Traffic Act 1988 (c 52) for the purposes of a test under subsection (1) of that section.

Power to control traffic for purposes of escorting a load of exceptional dimensions

9(1) A person whose accreditation specifies that this paragraph applies to him shall have, for the purpose of escorting a vehicle or trailer carrying a load of exceptional dimensions either to or from the relevant police area, the power of a constable engaged in the regulation of traffic in a road–

(a) to direct a vehicle to stop;

(b) to make a vehicle proceed in, or keep to, a particular line of traffic; and

(c) to direct pedestrians to stop.

(2) Sections 35 and 37 of the Road Traffic Act 1988 (offences of failing to comply with directions of constable engaged in regulation of traffic in a road) shall have effect in relation to the exercise of those powers for the purpose mentioned in sub-paragraph (1) by a person whose accreditation specifies that this paragraph applies to him as if the references to a constable engaged in regulation of traffic in a road were references to that person.

(3) The powers conferred by virtue of this paragraph may be exercised in any police area in England and Wales.

(4) In this paragraph 'vehicle or trailer carrying a load of exceptional dimensions' means a vehicle or trailer the use of which is authorised by an order made by the Secretary of State under section 44(1)(d) of the Road Traffic Act 1988.

Meaning of 'relevant police area'

10   In this Schedule 'the relevant police area', in relation to an accredited person, means the police area for which the police force whose chief officer granted his accreditation is maintained.

APPENDIX 5

THE PRIVATE SECURITY INDUSTRY ACT 2001 –
A BASIC OVERVIEW OF ITS KEY PROVISIONS

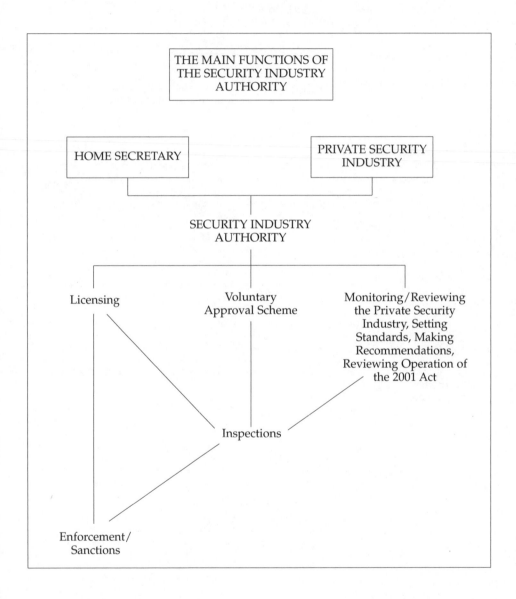

Who should be licensed? An overview

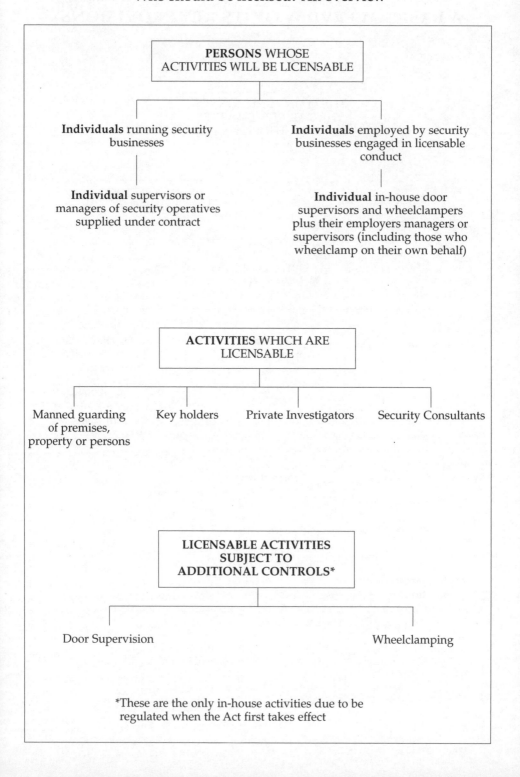

APPENDIX 6

TEXT OF THE PRIVATE SECURITY
INDUSTRY ACT 2001

The Security Industry Authority

1   The Security Industry Authority

(1) There shall be a body corporate to be known as the Security Industry Authority (in this Act referred to as 'the Authority').

(2) The functions of the Authority shall be–

   (a) to carry out the functions relating to licensing and approvals that are conferred on it by this Act;

   (b) to keep under review generally the provision of security industry services and other services involving the activities of security operatives;

   (c) for the purpose of protecting the public, to monitor the activities and effectiveness of persons carrying on businesses providing any such services as are mentioned in paragraph (b);

   (d) to ensure the carrying out of such inspections as it considers necessary of the activities and businesses of–

      (i)   persons engaged in licensable conduct; and

      (ii) persons registered under section 14 as approved providers of security industry services;

   (e) to set or approve standards of conduct, training and levels of supervision for adoption by–

      (i)   those who carry on businesses providing security industry services or other services involving the activities of security operatives; and

      (ii) those who are employed for the purposes of such businesses;

   (f) to make recommendations and proposals for the maintenance and improvement of standards in the provision of security industry services and other services involving the activities of security operatives;

   (g) to keep under review the operation of this Act.

(3) The Authority may do anything that it considers is calculated to facilitate, or is incidental or conducive to, the carrying out of any of its functions.

(4) Without prejudice to subsection (3), the Authority may, for any purpose connected with the carrying out of its functions–

   (a) make proposals to the Secretary of State for the modification of any provision contained in or made under this Act; and

   (b) undertake, or arrange for or support (whether financially or otherwise), the carrying out of research relating to the provision of security industry services and of other services involving the activities of security operatives.

(5) The Authority shall not be regarded–

   (a) as the servant or agent of the Crown; or

   (b) as enjoying any status, immunity or privilege of the Crown;

   and the property of the Authority shall not be regarded as property of, or property held on behalf of, the Crown.

(6) Schedule 1 (which makes provision about the Authority) shall have effect.

2   Directions etc by the Secretary of State

(1) In carrying out its functions the Authority shall comply with any general or specific directions given to it in writing by the Secretary of State.

(2) Before giving directions under subsection (1), the Secretary of State shall consult the Authority.

(3) The Authority shall provide the Secretary of State with such information about its activities as he may request.

Licence requirement

3   Conduct prohibited without a licence

(1) Subject to the following provisions of this Act, it shall be an offence for a person to engage in any licensable conduct except under and in accordance with a licence.

(2) For the purposes of this Act a person engages in licensable conduct if–

  (a) he carries out any designated activities for the purposes of, or in connection with, any contract for the supply of services under which–

  (i) he,

  (ii) a body corporate of which he is a director, or

  (iii) a firm of which he is a partner,

  is or may be required to secure that any such activities are carried out;

  (b) in the course of any employment of his by any person he carries out any designated activities for the purposes of, or in connection with, any contract for the supply of services under which his employer is or may be so required;

  (c) he carries out any designated activities in accordance with directions given to him by or on behalf of a person to whom his services are supplied (whether or not for the carrying out of any such activities) by–

  (i)   a body corporate of which he is a director,

  (ii) a firm of which he is a partner,

  (iii) a person by whom he is employed, or

  (iv) a person to whom he supplies his services under a contract for the purposes of which, or in connection with which, he is or may be required to work in accordance with the directions of another;

  (d) he acts–

  (i)   in the course of any employment of his by any person, or

  (ii) in accordance with any directions given as mentioned in paragraph (c),

  as the manager or supervisor of one or more individuals required in the course of their employment to engage in licensable conduct falling within paragraph (b);

  (e) he acts–

  (i)   in the course of any employment of his by any person, or

  (ii) in accordance with any directions given as mentioned in paragraph (c),

  as the manager or supervisor of individuals who are required in accordance with any such directions to engage in conduct which would be licensable conduct falling within paragraph (b) if they were required to engage in that conduct as the employees of the person to whom their services are supplied;

  (f) he is the director of any body corporate or the partner of any firm at a time when another of the directors or partners of the body or firm, or any employee of the body or firm, engages in licensable conduct falling within any of paragraphs (a) to (e);

(g) he is the employer of an individual who in the course of any employment of his with that employer carries out any designated activities subject to additional controls;

(h) in the course of any employment of his, or for purposes connected with his being a director or partner of a body corporate or firm, he carries out designated activities subject to additional controls;

(i) in the course of any employment of his by any person he acts as the manager or supervisor of one or more individuals the duties of whose employment involve the carrying out of any designated activities subject to additional controls; or

(j) in circumstances in which it is proposed to impose a charge for the release of immobilised vehicles, he carries out on his own behalf or on behalf of another person any designated activities consisting in activities to which paragraph 3 of Schedule 2 (immobilisation of vehicles) applies.

(3) In this Act 'designated activities' means such of the activities of a security operative as are for the time being designated for the purposes of this section by an order made by the Secretary of State; and an order under this subsection may designate different activities for the purposes of different paragraphs of subsection (2).

(4) For the purposes of this section a person shall not be treated as acting as the manager or supervisor of an individual by reason only of his giving directions to that individual in a case in which–

(a) the directions are given on behalf of a person to whom the individual's services are provided under a contract for services; and

(b) the person who under the contract provides the individual's services or another person acting on his behalf, acts as the manager or supervisor of that individual in relation to the activities carried out by him in accordance with those directions.

(5) Schedule 2 (which defines the activities that are to be treated as the activities of a security operative for the purposes of this Act and those which, so far as they are designated, are subject to additional controls) shall have effect.

(6) A person guilty of an offence under this section shall be liable, on summary conviction, to imprisonment for a term not exceeding six months or to a fine not exceeding level 5 on the standard scale, or to both.

4   Exemptions from licensing requirement

(1) If–

(a) it appears to the Secretary of State that there are circumstances in which licensable conduct is engaged in only by persons to whom suitable alternative arrangements will apply; and

(b) the Secretary of State is satisfied that, as a consequence, it is unnecessary for persons engaging in any such conduct in those circumstances to be required to be licensed under this Act,

then he may by regulations prescribing those circumstances provide that a person shall not be guilty of an offence under section 3 in respect of any conduct engaged in by him in those circumstances.

(2) The provision that may be made by regulations under subsection (1) includes provision that a person is not to be guilty of an offence in respect of any conduct

which is engaged in by him in the course of his employment by, or otherwise under the direction of, a person who is certified by the Authority in accordance with the regulations to be a person who the Authority is satisfied will secure that suitable alternative arrangements apply.

(3) In subsections (1) and (2) references to suitable alternative arrangements are references to arrangements that the Secretary of State or, as the case may be, the Authority is satisfied are equivalent, for all practical purposes so far as the protection of the public is concerned, to those applying to persons applying for and granted licences.

(4) A person shall not be guilty of an offence under section 3 in respect of any activities of his as a security operative if–

(a) he carries out those activities in his capacity as the director of a body corporate, the partner of any firm or the employee of any person;

(b) he has applied to the Authority for the grant of a licence and that application is pending;

(c) the licence applied for would authorise him to carry out those activities and is not one he has previously been refused;

(d) the body, firm or, as the case may be, the employer is a person who is for the time being registered under section 14 as an approved provider of security industry services; and

(e) the Authority has given notice to the body, firm or employer that it has authorised that body, firm or employer to use directors, partners or employees whose applications are pending to carry out activities that consist in or include those activities.

(5) Subsection (4) shall apply in the case of a person who carries out activities under directions given by or on behalf of another person in pursuance of a contract for the supply of the services of the first person as if the first person were an employee of the other one.

5   Offence of using unlicensed security operative

(1) A person is guilty of an offence if–

(a) he provides any security industry services to another;

(b) those services are provided wholly or partly by means of the activities of an individual as a security operative; and

(c) that individual's activities in connection with the provision of those services involve his engaging in licensable conduct in respect of which he is not the holder of a licence.

(2) In proceedings against any person for an offence under this section it shall be a defence for that person to show either–

(a) that he did not know, and had no reasonable grounds for suspecting, at the time when the activities were carried out, that the individual in question was not the holder of a licence in respect of those activities; or

(b) that he took all reasonable steps, in relation to the services in question, for securing that that individual would not engage in any licensable conduct in respect of which he was not the holder of a licence.

(3) A person shall not be guilty of an offence under this section in respect of any services in so far as those services are provided by means of conduct in which a person who is not the holder of a licence is entitled to engage by virtue of section 4.

(4) A person guilty of an offence under this section shall be liable–

(a) on summary conviction, to imprisonment for a term not exceeding six months or to a fine not exceeding the statutory maximum, or to both;

(b) on conviction on indictment, to imprisonment for a term not exceeding five years or to a fine, or to both.

6   Offence of using unlicensed wheel-clampers

(1) A person who is an occupier of any premises is guilty of an offence if–

(a) any individual carries out, in relation to vehicles on those premises, any designated activities consisting in activities to which paragraph 3 of Schedule 2 (immobilisation of vehicles) applies;

(b) the carrying out of those activities involves that individual's engaging in licensable conduct in respect of which he is not the holder of a licence; and

(c) those activities are carried out with the permission of that occupier or for the purposes of, or in connection with, any contract for the supply of services to him.

(2) In proceedings against any person for an offence under this section it shall be a defence for that person to show either–

(a) that he did not know, and had no reasonable grounds for suspecting, at the time when the activities were carried out, that the individual in question was not the holder of a licence in respect of those activities; or

(b) that he took all reasonable steps, in relation to the carrying out of those activities, for securing that that individual would not engage in any licensable conduct in respect of which he was not the holder of a licence.

(3) A person shall not be guilty of an offence under this section in respect of the carrying out of activities which are comprised in any conduct of an individual in which he is entitled to engage by virtue of section 4.

(4) A person guilty of an offence under this section shall be liable–

(a) on summary conviction, to imprisonment for a term not exceeding six months or to a fine not exceeding the statutory maximum, or to both;

(b) on conviction on indictment, to imprisonment for a term not exceeding five years or to a fine, or to both.

Licensing functions of the Authority

7   Licensing criteria

(1) It shall be the duty of the Authority, before granting any licences, to prepare and publish a document setting out–

(a) the criteria which it proposes to apply in determining whether or not to grant a licence; and

(b) the criteria which it proposes to apply in exercising its powers under this Act to revoke or modify a licence.

(2) The Authority may from time to time revise the document for the time being setting out the criteria mentioned in subsection (1)(a) and (b); and, if it does so, it shall publish the revised document.

(3) The criteria set out by the Authority under this section–

(a) shall include such criteria as the Authority considers appropriate for securing that the persons who engage in licensable conduct are fit and proper persons to engage in such conduct;

(b) may include such criteria as the Authority considers appropriate for securing that those persons have the training and skills necessary to engage in the conduct for which they are licensed; and

(c) may also include criteria relating to such other matters as the Authority thinks fit.

(4) In setting out any criteria or revised criteria under this section the Authority may provide for different criteria to apply–

(a) in relation to licences for different descriptions of licensable conduct; and

(b) in relation to the initial grant of a licence and in relation to a further grant to the same licensee for the purpose of renewing an earlier licence.

(5) Criteria or revised criteria set out under this section shall not have effect for the purposes of this Act unless the Secretary of State has approved them.

(6) The publication in accordance with this section of any document setting out any criteria or revised criteria must be in such manner as the Authority considers appropriate for bringing it to the attention of the persons likely to be affected by it.

8   Licences to engage in licensable conduct

(1) The Authority may, on an application made to it, grant to the applicant a licence to engage in any such licensable conduct as may be described in the licence.

(2) An application to the Authority for the grant of a licence–

(a) must be in such form, and

(b) must be accompanied by such information,

as may be prescribed.

(3) In determining whether or not to grant a licence the Authority shall apply the criteria for the time being applicable under section 7.

(4) The Authority may refuse to grant a licence until–

(a) it has been satisfied as to the identity of the applicant in such manner as may be prescribed;

(b) the applicant has supplemented his application with such further information (if any) as the Authority may request after receiving the application; and

(c) the Authority has been able to carry out such further inquiries (if any) in relation to the applicant as it considers appropriate.

(5) A licence granted by the Authority to engage in any description of licensable conduct–

(a) must be in such form,

(b) must contain such information, and

(c) must be granted on such conditions,

as may be prescribed in relation to licences to engage in that description of licensable conduct.

(6) Such a licence may be granted subject to such conditions, in addition to the prescribed conditions, as the Authority considers appropriate in relation to the licence in question.

(7) On the making of an application for the grant of a licence, the applicant shall pay to the Authority such fee as may be prescribed.

(8) Subject to section 10, a licence shall remain in force–

(a) except in a case to which paragraph (b) applies, for a period of three years beginning with the day on which it is granted; and

(b) in any case for which provision as to the duration of the licence is made by the Secretary of State by order, for such other period beginning with that day as may be specified in the order.

9   Licence conditions

(1) The power of the Secretary of State to prescribe the conditions on which a licence must be granted and the power of the Authority to impose additional conditions for such a licence shall include power to prescribe or impose–

(a) conditions containing requirements as to the training, registration and insurances which the licensee is to undergo, or to maintain, while the licence remains in force;

(b) conditions as to the manner in which the licensee is to carry out specified activities of a security operative that he is licensed to carry out;

(c) conditions imposing obligations as to the production and display of the licence;

(d) conditions imposing obligations as to the information to be provided from time to time by the licensee to the Authority; and

(e) such other conditions (whether or not relating to the criteria that would be applied by the Authority in determining whether to grant the licence) as the Secretary of State or the Authority thinks fit.

(2) The conditions that may be prescribed or imposed in relation to any description of licence may include conditions imposing obligations on a licensee by reference to requirements made or directions given by the Authority.

(3) In relation to a licence authorising licensable conduct falling within subsection (2)(g) of section 3, the references in subsection (1) of this section to the licensee include references to any of his employees who carry out any designated activities subject to additional controls.

(4) Any person who contravenes the conditions of any licence granted to him shall be guilty of an offence and liable, on summary conviction, to a term of imprisonment not exceeding six months or to a fine not exceeding level 5 on the standard scale, or to both.

(5) In proceedings against any person for an offence under subsection (4) it shall be a defence for that person to show that he exercised all due diligence to avoid a contravention of the conditions of the licence.

10   Revocation and modification of licences

(1) The Authority may by notice in writing to the licensee modify or revoke any licence granted to him (including any of the conditions of that licence).

(2) In determining whether or not to modify or revoke a licence, the Authority shall apply the criteria for the time being applicable under section 7.

(3) The modifications that may be made under this section include one suspending the effect of the licence for such period as the Authority may determine.

11   Appeals in licensing matters

(1) Where–

(a) an application for a licence is refused,

(b) a licence is granted subject to conditions imposed under section 8(6), or

(c) a licence is modified or revoked,

the applicant or, as the case may be, the holder of the licence may appeal to the appropriate magistrates' court against the Authority's decision to refuse to grant the licence, to impose those conditions or, as the case may be, to modify or to revoke the licence.

(2) An appeal under subsection (1) must be brought before the end of the period of twenty-one days beginning with the day on which the decision appealed against was first notified to the appellant by the Authority.

(3) For the purposes of subsection (1) the appropriate magistrates' court is the magistrates' court for the petty sessions area in which is situated, as the case may be–

(a) the address for the appellant that has been supplied for the purpose of being recorded (if a licence is granted) in the register maintained under section 12; or

(b) the address for the appellant that is for the time being recorded in that register.

(4) Where a magistrates' court makes a decision on an appeal under subsection (1), an appeal to the Crown Court may be brought against that decision either by the Authority or by the person on whose appeal that decision was made.

(5) A court to which an appeal is brought under this section shall determine the appeal in accordance with the criteria for the time being applicable under section 7.

(6) Where an application for the grant of a licence by way of a renewal is refused or a licence is revoked, the licence to which the application or revocation relates shall be deemed to remain in force–

(a) for the period during which an appeal may be brought under subsection (1);

(b) for the period from the bringing of any such appeal until it is determined or abandoned;

(c) for the period from any determination on appeal that a licence should be granted until effect is given to that determination, or it is overturned on a further appeal;

(d) during any such period as the appropriate magistrates' court or the Crown Court may direct, pending an appeal from a determination made on an appeal to that magistrates' court.

12 Register of licences

(1) It shall be the duty of the Authority to establish and maintain a register of persons licensed under this Act.

(2) The Authority shall secure that the register contains particulars of every person who for the time being holds a licence.

(3) The particulars that must be recorded in every entry in the register relating to the holder of a licence are–

(a) the name of the holder of the licence;

(b) an address for the holder of the licence which satisfies the prescribed requirements;

(c) the time when the licence will cease to have effect unless renewed; and

(d) the terms and other conditions of his licence.

(4) It shall be the duty of the Authority to ensure that such arrangements are in force as it considers appropriate for–

    (a) allowing members of the public and such other persons as it thinks fit to inspect the contents of the register; and

    (b) securing that such publicity is given to any modification or revocation of a licence as will bring it to the attention of persons likely to be interested in it.

(5) The Authority may impose such fee as it considers reasonable for allowing a person to inspect the register or to take a copy of any part of it.

13   Licensing at local authority level

(1) The Secretary of State may by order make provision for local authorities to carry out some or all of the Authority's relevant licensing functions in relation to such cases and such areas, and for such purposes, as may be specified or described in the order.

(2) References in this section to the Authority's relevant licensing functions are references to such of its functions under this Act (other than section 7) as relate to the grant, revocation or modification of licences to engage in any such licensable conduct as will or may involve, or relate to, the carrying out of activities to which paragraph 8 of Schedule 2 (door supervisors etc for public houses and clubs and comparable venues) applies.

(3) An order under this section may–

    (a) impose such conditions and requirements in respect of the carrying out of any of the Authority's relevant licensing functions by a local authority as the Secretary of State thinks fit;

    (b) provide for any of those conditions or requirements to be framed by reference to directions given by the Secretary of State in accordance with the order;

    (c) provide for any of the powers exercisable by a local authority by virtue of such an order to be exercisable concurrently in relation to the same case by the Authority and that local authority; and

    (d) authorise a local authority to retain any fee paid to them by virtue of section 8(7).

(4) Section 11 shall apply in relation to a decision made by a local authority in accordance with an order under subsection (1) as it applies in relation to a decision of the Authority; and where it so applies it shall have effect as if the references in subsections (2) and (4) of that section to the Authority were a reference to the local authority that made the decision in question.

(5) The Secretary of State may by order make such provision repealing or modifying the provisions of any local enactment as he considers appropriate in consequence of the coming into force of any of the provisions of this Act or of an order under subsection (1).

(6) The Secretary of State shall consult the Authority before making an order under this section.

(7) In this section 'local authority' means–

    (a) the council for any county or district in England other than a metropolitan county the districts comprised in which are districts for which there are councils;

    (b) the council for any London borough;

    (c) the Common Council of the City of London;

    (d) the Council of the Isles of Scilly;

    (e) the council for any county or county borough in Wales.

Approved contractors

14 Register of approved contractors

(1) It shall be the duty of the Authority to establish and maintain a register of approved providers of security industry services.

(2) The Authority shall secure that the register contains particulars of every person who is for the time being approved under any arrangements in force under section 15.

(3) The particulars that must be recorded in every entry in the register relating to an approved person are–

   (a) the name of that person;

   (b) an address for that person which satisfies the prescribed requirements;

   (c) the services in respect of which that person is approved;

   (d) the time when the approval will cease to have effect unless renewed; and

   (e) the conditions of the approval.

(4) It shall be the duty of the Authority to ensure that such arrangements are in force as it considers appropriate for–

   (a) allowing members of the public to inspect the contents of the register; and

   (b) securing that such publicity is given to any modification or withdrawal of an approval as will bring it to the attention of persons likely to be interested in it.

(5) The Authority may impose such fee as it considers reasonable for allowing a person to inspect the register or to take a copy of any part of it.

15 Arrangements for the grant of approvals

(1) It shall be the duty of the Authority to secure that there are arrangements in force for granting approvals to persons who–

   (a) are providing security industry services in England and Wales; and

   (b) seek approval in respect of any such services that they are providing, or are proposing to provide.

(2) The arrangements must–

   (a) allow for an approval to be granted either in respect of all the services in respect of which it is sought or in respect of only some of them;

   (b) ensure that an approval is granted to a person in respect of any services only if the condition for the grant of an approval is satisfied in accordance with subsection (3);

   (c) provide for an approval granted to any person to have effect subject to such conditions (whether or not connected with the provision of the services in respect of which the approval is granted) as may be contained in the approval;

   (d) enable a person to whom the Authority is proposing to grant an approval to refuse it if the proposal is in different terms from the approval which was sought;

   (e) make provision for the handling of complaints and disputes which–

      (i) are required by the conditions of an approved person's approval to be dealt with in accordance with a procedure maintained by him in pursuance of those conditions; but

      (ii) are not disposed of by the application of that procedure;

(f) provide for an approval to cease to have effect (unless renewed)–

  (i) except in a case to which sub-paragraph (ii) applies, at the end of the period of three years beginning with the day on which it is granted; and

  (ii) in a case for which provision as to the duration of the approval is made by the Secretary of State by order, for such other period beginning with that day as may be specified in the order;

(g) provide for the modification and withdrawal of approvals.

(3) The condition that must be fulfilled before an approval is granted to any person is that the Authority is satisfied that he–

  (a) will comply, in providing the services in respect of which he is approved, with such technical and other requirements as may be prescribed;

  (b) is a person in relation to whom such other requirements as may be prescribed are, and will continue to be, satisfied;

  (c) is, and will continue to be, able and willing to comply with any requirements that the Authority is proposing to impose by means of conditions of the approval; and

  (d) is otherwise a fit and proper person to be approved in respect of those services.

(4) Regulations made by virtue of paragraph (a) or (b) of subsection (3) may frame a requirement for the purposes of that subsection by reference to the opinion of a person specified in the regulations, or of a person chosen in a manner determined in accordance with the regulations.

(5) The requirements which (subject to subsection (6)) may be imposed by conditions contained in an approval in accordance with the arrangements include–

  (a) requirements to provide information to such persons, in such form, at such times and in response to such requests as may be specified in or determined under the terms of the condition;

  (b) requirements framed by reference to the opinion or directions of a person specified in or chosen in accordance with provision contained in the conditions.

(6) Nothing in the arrangements shall authorise the imposition, by conditions contained in an approval, of any requirements for–

  (a) the provision of information; or

  (b) the maintenance of a procedure for handling complaints or disputes,

in relation to any matter other than one appearing to the Authority to be relevant to the matters mentioned in subsection (3)(a) to (d).

(7) Any requirement to provide information that is imposed in accordance with the arrangements on any person by the conditions of his approval shall be enforceable at the suit or instance of the Authority.

(8) Where any arrangements under this section so provide, a person who–

  (a) seeks an approval under the arrangements;

  (b) applies for a modification of such an approval;

  (c) is for the time being approved under the arrangements; or

  (d) has his approval under the arrangements modified wholly or partly in consequence of an application made by him,

shall pay to the Authority, at such time or times as may be prescribed, such fee or fees as may be prescribed in relation to that time or those times.

16   Right to use approved status

(1) The Authority may approve the terms in which a person who is for the time being registered under section 14 as an approved provider of security industry services may hold himself out as so registered.

(2) A person is guilty of an offence if–

  (a) he holds himself out as registered under section 14 as an approved provider of any security industry services when he is not so registered; or

  (b) he is so registered but holds himself out as so registered in terms that have not been approved by the Authority in relation to his case.

(3) A person guilty of an offence under this section shall be liable–

  (a) on summary conviction, to a fine not exceeding the statutory maximum;

  (b) on conviction on indictment, to a fine.

(4) For the purposes of this section references in this section to a person's holding himself out as registered as an approved provider of any services include references to his holding himself out to be a person who is for the time being approved in respect of those services in accordance with arrangements under section 15.

17   Imposition of requirements for approval

(1) The Secretary of State may by regulations provide that persons of prescribed descriptions are to be prohibited from providing prescribed security industry services unless they are for the time being approved in respect of those services in accordance with arrangements under section 15.

(2) A person is guilty of an offence if he contravenes any prohibition imposed on him by regulations under subsection (1).

(3) A person who–

  (a) is approved in respect of any security industry services in accordance with arrangements under section 15, and

  (b) would be prohibited by regulations under subsection (1) from providing those services except while for the time being so approved,

  is guilty of an offence if he contravenes any of the conditions of his approval in respect of those services.

(4) A person guilty of an offence under this section is liable–

  (a) on summary conviction, to a fine not exceeding the statutory maximum;

  (b) on conviction on indictment, to a fine.

(5) The Secretary of State may by regulations make provision in relation to cases in which a person is required by regulations under subsection (1) to be approved in respect of any services in accordance with arrangements under section 15–

  (a) for the conditions that are to be contained in his approval in relation to the handling of complaints made about the provision of those services; and

  (b) generally in relation to the arrangements under that section that are to be made for such cases.

18   Appeals relating to approvals

(1) Where–

  (a) an application for an approval for the purposes of section 15 is refused,

  (b) conditions are included as conditions of such an approval, or

  (c) such an approval is modified or withdrawn,

the applicant or, as the case may be, the approved person may appeal to the appropriate magistrates' court against the Authority's decision to refuse to grant the approval, to include those conditions or, as the case may be, to modify or to withdraw the approval.

(2) An appeal under subsection (1) must be brought before the end of the period of twenty-one days beginning with the day on which the decision appealed against was first notified to the appellant by the Authority.

(3) For the purposes of subsection (1) the appropriate magistrates' court is the magistrates' court for the petty sessions area in which is situated, as the case may be–

  (a) the address for the appellant that has been supplied for the purpose of being recorded (if an approval is granted) in the register maintained under section 14; or

  (b) the address for the appellant that is for the time being recorded in that register.

(4) Where a magistrates' court makes a decision on an appeal under subsection (1), an appeal to the Crown Court may be brought against that decision either by the Authority or by the person on whose appeal that decision was made.

(5) Where an application for the grant of an approval by way of a renewal is refused or an approval is withdrawn, the approval to which the application or withdrawal relates shall be deemed to remain in force–

  (a) for the period during which an appeal may be brought under subsection (1);

  (b) for the period from the bringing of any such appeal until it is determined or abandoned;

  (c) for the period from any determination on appeal that an approval should be granted until effect is given to that determination, or it is overturned on a further appeal;

  (d) during any such period as the appropriate magistrates' court or the Crown Court may direct, pending an appeal from a determination made on an appeal to that magistrates' court.

Entry, inspection and information

19 Powers of entry and inspection

(1) Subject to subsections (3) and (4), a person authorised in writing for the purpose by the Authority may enter any premises owned or occupied by any person appearing to him to be a regulated person other than premises occupied exclusively for residential purposes as a private dwelling.

(2) A person authorised in writing for the purpose by the Authority may require any person appearing to him to be a regulated person to produce to him any documents or other information relating to any matter connected with–

  (a) any licensable conduct which has been or may be engaged in by the person so appearing;

  (b) the provision by the person so appearing of any security industry services;

  (c) any matters in respect of which conditions are imposed on the person so appearing by virtue of a licence or of an approval granted in accordance with arrangements under section 15.

(3) A person exercising the power conferred by subsection (1) shall do so only at a reasonable hour.

(4) A person exercising such a power shall–

    (a) comply with any reasonable request made (whether before or after entry is gained to the premises) by any person present on the premises to do any one or more of the following–

        (i)   state the purpose for which the power is being exercised;

        (ii) show the authorisation by the Authority for his exercise of the power;

        (iii) produce evidence of his identity;

    (b) make a record of the date and time of his entry, the period for which he remained there and his conduct while there; and

    (c) if requested to do so by any person present on the premises at the time of the entry, provide that person with a copy of that record.

(5) A person is guilty of an offence if–

    (a) he intentionally obstructs any person in the exercise of any power conferred by subsection (1);

    (b) he fails, without reasonable excuse, to comply with any requirement imposed by subsection (2); or

    (c) he makes an unauthorised disclosure of any information obtained by him in the exercise of any power conferred by this section, or as a consequence of the exercise of any such power by another.

(6) For the purposes of this section a disclosure of information obtained by any person as mentioned in subsection (5)(c) is authorised if, and only if, it is made–

    (a) for the purposes of the carrying out by the Authority of any of its functions under this Act; or

    (b) for the purposes of any criminal proceedings.

(7) A person guilty of an offence under this section shall be liable, on summary conviction, to a term of imprisonment not exceeding six months or to a fine not exceeding level 5 on the standard scale, or to both.

(8) In this section 'regulated person' means–

    (a) the holder of any licence granted under this Act;

    (b) any person who engages in licensable conduct without being the holder of a licence under this Act;

    (c) any person who is for the time being approved in accordance with arrangements under section 15 in respect of any services which regulations under section 17 prohibit him from providing unless so approved; or

    (d) any person who is not so approved but provides security industry services which he is prohibited by any such regulations from providing.

20 Guidance as to exercise of power of entry

(1) It shall be the duty of the Authority to prepare and publish a document containing its guidance as to the manner in which persons authorised to enter premises under subsection (1) of section 19 should–

    (a) exercise the power conferred by that subsection; and

    (b) conduct themselves after entering premises in exercise of that power.

(2) The Authority may from time to time revise the guidance published under this section; and, if it does so, it shall publish the revised guidance.

(3) A requirement under this section for the Authority to publish guidance or revised guidance shall be a requirement to publish it in such manner as appears to the Authority appropriate for bringing it to the attention of persons likely to be affected by it.

21 Access to enhanced criminal records certificates

In section 115(5) of the Police Act 1997 (c. 50) (matters in respect of which an enhanced criminal record certificate may be required), after paragraph (g) there shall be inserted–

'(ga) a licence under the Private Security Industry Act 2001 to engage in any such licensable conduct (within the meaning of that Act) as will or may involve, or relate to, activities to which paragraph 8 of Schedule 2 to that Act applies (door supervisors etc for public houses and clubs and comparable venues).'

22 False information

(1) A person is guilty of an offence if for any purposes connected with the carrying out by the Authority of any of its functions under this Act–

(a) he makes any statement to the Authority which he knows to be false in a material particular; or

(b) he recklessly makes any statement to the Authority which is false in a material particular.

(2) A person guilty of an offence under this section shall be liable, on summary conviction, to imprisonment for a term not exceeding six months or to a fine not exceeding level 5 on the standard scale, or to both.

Supplemental

23 Criminal liability of directors etc

Where an offence under any provision of this Act is committed by a body corporate and is proved to have been committed with the consent or connivance of, or to be attributable to any neglect on the part of–

(a) a director, manager, secretary or other similar officer of the body corporate, or

(b) any person who was purporting to act in any such capacity,

he (as well as the body corporate) shall be guilty of that offence and liable to be proceeded against and punished accordingly.

24 Orders and regulations

(1) In this Act 'prescribed' means prescribed by regulations made by the Secretary of State, or determined in any such manner and by such person as may be provided for in any such regulations; and 'prescribe' shall be construed accordingly.

(2) Every power of the Secretary of State under this Act to make an order or regulations shall be exercisable by statutory instrument.

(3) A statutory instrument containing any order or regulations made under any provision of this Act, other than one containing either–

(a) an order under section 26(2); or

(b) an order a draft of which has been approved for the purposes of paragraph 1(3) or 7(3) of Schedule 2,

shall be subject to annulment in pursuance of a resolution of either House of Parliament.

(4) Before–

    (a) making any regulations under any provision of this Act,

    (b) making any order under any provision of this Act other than paragraph 1(2) or 7(2) of Schedule 2, or

    (c) laying any draft order under paragraph 1(2) or 7(2) of Schedule 2 before Parliament,

the Secretary of State shall consult the Authority.

(5) Any order or regulations made under any of the preceding provisions of this Act or any provision contained in a Schedule to this Act may–

    (a) make different provisions for different cases;

    (b) contain such incidental, supplemental, consequential and transitional provision as the Secretary of State thinks fit.

25 Interpretation

(1) In this Act–

'activities of a security operative' shall be construed in accordance with Part 1 of Schedule 2;

'activities subject to additional controls' shall be construed in accordance with Part 2 of that Schedule;

'the Authority' means the Security Industry Authority;

'contravention' includes a failure to comply, and cognate expressions shall be construed accordingly;

'designated activities' has the meaning given by section 3(3);

'director'–

    (a) in relation to a company (within the meaning of the Companies Act 1985 (c. 6)), includes a shadow director;

    (b) in relation to any such company that is a subsidiary of another, includes any director or shadow director of the other company; and

    (c) in relation to a body corporate whose affairs are managed by its members, means a member of that body corporate;

'information' includes reports, references and other documents, photographs and data of any description;

'licence' means a licence from the Authority under this Act;

'licensable conduct' shall be construed in accordance with section 3(2);

'local statutory provision' means–

    (a) a provision of any local Act;

    (b) a provision of any instrument in the nature of a local enactment;

    (c) a provision of any instrument made under a local statutory provision;

'modification' includes amendments, additions and omissions, and cognate expressions shall be construed accordingly;

'motor vehicle' means a mechanically propelled vehicle or a vehicle designed or adapted for towing by a mechanically propelled vehicle;

'premises' includes any vehicle or moveable structure and any other place whatever, whether or not occupied as land;

'relevant accountancy body' means any of the following–

(a) the Institute of Chartered Accountants in England and Wales;

(b) the Institute of Chartered Accountants of Scotland;

(c) the Institute of Chartered Accountants in Ireland;

(d) the Association of Chartered Certified Accountants;

(e) the Chartered Institute of Management Accountants;

(f) the Chartered Institute of Public Finance and Accountancy;

'security industry services' means services which are provided under a contract for services and in the course of which the person providing the services secures–

(a) that the activities of a security operative are carried out; or

(b) that a person is made available to carry out, under directions given by or on behalf of another person, any activities which will or are likely to consist of or include the activities of a security operative;

'surveillance' includes covertly listening to or recording conversations or other sounds and any method of covertly obtaining information;

'shadow director' means a shadow director as defined in section 741(2) of the Companies Act 1985;

'subsidiary' means a subsidiary as defined in section 736 of the Companies Act 1985 (c. 6);

'vehicle' includes any vessel, aircraft or hovercraft.

(2) In this Act references, in relation to a firm, to a member of the firm include references to any person who, in relation to that firm, is liable as a partner under section 14 of the Partnership Act 1890 (c. 39) (persons liable by 'holding out').

26 Short title, commencement and extent

(1) This Act may be cited as the Private Security Industry Act 2001.

(2) The provisions of this Act, other than this section, shall come into force on such day as the Secretary of State may by order made by statutory instrument appoint; and different days may be appointed under this subsection for different purposes.

(3) This Act extends to the United Kingdom for the purposes only of–

(a) the amendment of the Police Act 1997 (c. 50) by section 21; and

(b) the amendments by Schedule 1 of the following enactments–

(i) the Public Records Act 1958 (c. 51);

(ii) the Parliamentary Commissioner Act 1967 (c. 13);

(iii) the Superannuation Act 1972 (c. 11);

(iv) the House of Commons Disqualification Act 1975 (c. 24);

(v) the Northern Ireland Assembly Disqualification Act 1975 (c. 25); and

(vi) the Freedom of Information Act 2000 (c. 36).

(4) Subject to subsection (3), this Act extends to England and Wales only.

SCHEDULES
SCHEDULE 1
THE SECURITY INDUSTRY AUTHORITY

Membership and chairman

1(1) The Authority shall consist of such number of members as the Secretary of State may determine.

(2) The appointment of a person to be a member shall be made by the Secretary of State.

(3) The Secretary of State shall appoint one of the members of the Authority to be its chairman.

Tenure of office

2(1) Subject to the provisions of this Schedule, a member shall hold and vacate office in accordance with the terms of his appointment.

(2) A person shall not be appointed as a member for more than five years.

(3) A person may at any time resign his office as a member by notice in writing to the Secretary of State.

(4) A person appointed as chairman of the Authority–

   (a) shall hold and vacate that office in accordance with the terms of his appointment;

   (b) may resign that office by notice in writing to the Secretary of State; and

   (c) shall cease to hold that office if he ceases to be a member.

3   The Secretary of State may remove a person from office as a member or as chairman of the Authority if satisfied that–

   (a) he has without reasonable excuse failed, for a continuous period of three months, to carry out his functions as a member or (as the case may be) as chairman;

   (b) he has without reasonable excuse been absent from three consecutive meetings of the Authority;

   (c) he has been convicted (whether before or after his appointment) of a criminal offence;

   (d) he is an undischarged bankrupt or his estate has been sequestrated and he has not been discharged, or he has made an arrangement with, or granted a trust deed for, his creditors;

   (e) he has failed to comply with the terms of his appointment; or

   (f) he is otherwise unable or unfit to carry out his functions as a member or (as the case may be) as chairman.

4   A person who ceases (otherwise than by virtue of paragraph 3) to be a member or to be the chairman of the Authority shall be eligible for re-appointment.

Remuneration, pensions etc of members

5(1) The Authority shall pay to its members such remuneration and allowances as the Secretary of State may determine.

(2) The Authority shall, as regards any of its members or former members in whose case the Secretary of State may so determine, pay or make payments in respect of such pension or gratuity as the Secretary of State may determine.

(3) If–

    (a) a person ceases to be a member or ceases to be the chairman of the Authority, and

    (b) it appears to the Secretary of State that there are special circumstances which make it right that he should receive compensation,

the Secretary of State may direct the Authority to make a payment of such amount as he may determine.

Staff etc

6(1) The Authority shall have–

    (a) a chief executive, with responsibility to the Authority for the carrying out of its functions and the management of its employees; and

    (b) subject to the approval of the Secretary of State as to numbers and terms and conditions of service, such other employees as the Authority may appoint.

  (2) The first appointment of a chief executive shall be made by the Secretary of State; but, subject to obtaining the Secretary of State's consent to the appointment, every subsequent appointment of a chief executive shall be made by the Authority itself.

  (3) References in this Schedule to the employees of the Authority include references to its chief executive (whether appointed by the Secretary of State or by the Authority).

7(1) The Authority shall pay to its employees such remuneration and allowances as it may, with the consent of the Secretary of State, determine.

  (2) The Authority shall–

    (a) pay, or make payments in respect of, such pensions or gratuities to or in respect of its employees or former employees as it may, with the consent of the Secretary of State, determine; and

    (b) provide and maintain such schemes (whether contributory or not) as it may determine, with the consent of the Secretary of State, for the payment of pensions or gratuities in respect of its employees or former employees.

  (3) References in this paragraph to pensions and gratuities include references to pensions or gratuities by way of compensation to or in respect of employees who suffer loss of employment or loss or diminution of emoluments.

  (4) If any person–

    (a) on ceasing to be employed by the Authority becomes or continues to be one of its members; and

    (b) was, by reference to his employment, a participant in a pension scheme maintained by the Authority,

the Authority may, with the consent of the Secretary of State, make provision for that person to continue to participate in that scheme, on such terms and conditions as it may with the consent of the Secretary of State determine, as if his service as a member were service as an employee.

  (5) Any provision made by virtue of sub-paragraph (4) is without prejudice to paragraph 5.

Committees

8(1) The Authority may establish committees.

  (2) Any committee established under sub-paragraph (1) may establish one or more sub-committees.

(3) A person who is not a member of the Authority may be appointed to a committee or sub-committee of the Authority.

(4) The Authority may pay to members of its committees or sub-committees who are neither members nor employees of the Authority such remuneration and allowances as the Secretary of State may determine.

Delegation to committees and staff

9(1) The Authority may, to such extent as it may determine, delegate any of its functions to any committee of the Authority or to any employee of the Authority.

(2) Any such committee may, to such extent as it may determine, delegate any function conferred on it to any of its sub-committees or to any employee of the Authority.

(3) Any sub-committee of the Authority may, to such extent as the sub-committee may determine, delegate any functions conferred on the sub-committee to any employee of the Authority.

Proceedings

10(1) Subject to the following provisions of this paragraph, the Authority may regulate–

    (a) its own procedure (including quorum); and

    (b) the procedure (including quorum) of its committees and sub-committees.

(2) The quorum for meetings of the Authority shall in the first instance be determined by a meeting of the Authority that is attended by at least five of its members.

(3) The Authority shall make provision for a quorum for meetings of its committees or sub-committees to include at least one member or employee of the Authority.

11 The validity of any proceedings of the Authority, or of any of its committees or sub-committees, shall not be affected by–

    (a) any vacancy among the members of the Authority or of members of the committee or sub-committee;

    (b) any vacancy in the office of the chairman of the Authority; or

    (c) any defect in the appointment of any one or more members or of the chairman of the Authority.

Application of seal and evidence

12 The application of the seal of the Authority shall be authenticated by the signature–

    (a) of any member; or

    (b) of any other person who has been authorised by the Authority (whether generally or specially) for that purpose.

13 A document purporting to be–

    (a) duly executed by the Authority under its seal; or

    (b) signed on its behalf,

shall be received in evidence and shall, unless the contrary is proved, be taken to be so executed or signed.

Money

14(1) The Secretary of State may make payments to the Authority out of money provided by Parliament.

(2) The Authority shall not borrow money except with the consent of the Secretary of State.

15(1) The Authority may impose such charges as it considers appropriate in connection with the carrying out of any of its functions.

(2) The Authority shall pay to the Secretary of State all sums received by it (otherwise than under paragraph 14) in the course of, or in connection with, the carrying out of its functions.

(3) Sub-paragraph (2) shall not apply where the Secretary of State so directs.

(4) Any sums received by the Secretary of State under sub-paragraph (2) shall be paid into the Consolidated Fund.

16(1) The Authority shall–

(a) keep proper accounts and proper records in relation to the accounts; and

(b) prepare a statement of accounts in respect of each financial year.

(2) The statement of accounts shall be in such form, and shall contain such information, as the Secretary of State may direct.

(3) The Authority shall, within such period after the end of each financial year as the Secretary of State may direct, send copies of the statement of accounts relating to that year to the Secretary of State and to the Comptroller and Auditor General.

(4) The Comptroller and Auditor General shall–

(a) examine, certify and report on every statement of accounts sent to him by the Authority under this paragraph; and

(b) lay copies of each such statement and of his report on it before each House of Parliament.

Annual report

17(1) As soon as practicable after the end of each financial year, the Authority shall send to the Secretary of State a report on the carrying out of its functions during that year.

(2) The Secretary of State shall lay a copy of each such report before each House of Parliament.

The Public Records Act 1958 (c. 51)

18 In Schedule 1 to the Public Records Act 1958 (definition of public records), in Part 2 of the Table at the end of paragraph 3 there shall be inserted, at the appropriate place–

'Security Industry Authority'.

The Parliamentary Commissioner Act 1967 (c. 13)

19 In Schedule 2 to the Parliamentary Commissioner Act 1967 (departments etc subject to investigation), there shall be inserted, at the appropriate place–

'Security Industry Authority'.

The Superannuation Act 1972 (c. 11)

20   In Schedule 1 to the Superannuation Act 1972 (kinds of employment to which that Act applies), in the entries under the heading 'Other bodies', there shall be inserted, at the appropriate place–

'The Security Industry Authority'.

The House of Commons Disqualification Act 1975 (c. 24)

21   In Part 2 of Schedule 1 to the House of Commons Disqualification Act 1975 (bodies whose members are disqualified) there shall be inserted, at the appropriate place–

'The Security Industry Authority'.

The Northern Ireland Assembly Disqualification Act 1975 (c. 25)

22   In Part 2 of Schedule 1 to the Northern Ireland Assembly Disqualification Act 1975 (bodies whose members are disqualified) there shall be inserted (at the appropriate place)–

'The Security Industry Authority'.

The Freedom of Information Act 2000 (c. 36)

23   In Part 6 of Schedule 1 to the Freedom of Information Act 2000 (bodies etc which are public authorities for the purposes of the Act) there shall be inserted (at the appropriate place)–

'The Security Industry Authority'.

Interpretation

24   In this Schedule–

'delegate' includes further delegate;

'financial year' means–

(a) the period beginning with the day appointed for the coming into force of section 1 and ending with the next 31st March; and

(b) any subsequent period of twelve months ending with 31st March; and

'member', except in so far as the context otherwise requires, means a member of the Authority.

SCHEDULE 2

ACTIVITIES LIABLE TO CONTROL UNDER THE ACT

PART 1

ACTIVITIES OF SECURITY OPERATIVES

General

1(1) Subject to sub-paragraph (2), the activities which are referred to in this Act as the activities of a security operative are those to which any one or more of the following paragraphs of this Part of this Schedule applies.

(2) The Secretary of State may by order amend this Part of this Schedule for the purpose of adding or excluding any such activities as he thinks fit to or from those that fall to be regarded for the purposes of this Act as the activities of a security operative.

(3) The Secretary of State shall not make an order containing (with or without any other provision) any provision authorised by sub-paragraph (2) unless a draft of the order has been laid before Parliament and approved by a resolution of each House.

Manned guarding

2(1) This paragraph applies (subject to the following provisions of this paragraph) to any of the following activities–

(a) guarding premises against unauthorised access or occupation, against outbreaks of disorder or against damage;

(b) guarding property against destruction or damage, against being stolen or against being otherwise dishonestly taken or obtained;

(c) guarding one or more individuals against assault or against injuries that might be suffered in consequence of the unlawful conduct of others.

(2) In this paragraph references to guarding premises against unauthorised access include references to being wholly or partly responsible for determining the suitability for admission to the premises of persons applying for admission.

(3) In this paragraph references to guarding against something happening include references to so providing a physical presence, or carrying out any form of patrol or surveillance, as–

(a) to deter or otherwise discourage it from happening; or

(b) to provide information, if it happens, about what has happened.

(4) This paragraph does not apply to the activities of an individual who exercises control over the persons allowed access to any premises to the extent only of securing, or checking, that persons allowed access–

(a) have paid for admission; or

(b) have invitations or passes allowing admission.

(5) This paragraph does not apply to the activities of a person who, incidentally to the carrying out of any activities in relation to a group of individuals which (disregarding this sub-paragraph) are neither–

(a) the activities of a security operative; nor

(b) activities comprising the exercise of any such control as is mentioned in sub-paragraph (4),

maintains order or discipline amongst those individuals.

(6) This paragraph does not apply to the activities of a person who, incidentally to the carrying out of activities which (disregarding this sub-paragraph) are not wholly or mainly the activities of a security operative, responds to a sudden or unexpected occurrence.

Immobilisation of vehicles

3(1) This paragraph applies (subject to the following provisions of this paragraph) to the immobilisation of a motor vehicle by the attachment to the vehicle, or to a part of it, of an immobilising device.

(2) This paragraph applies only to activities carried out for the purpose of preventing or inhibiting the removal of a vehicle by a person otherwise entitled to remove it.

(3) This paragraph does not apply to any activities carried out in relation to a vehicle while it is on a road within the meaning of the Road Traffic Act 1988 (c. 52).

Private investigations

4(1) This paragraph applies (subject to the following provisions of this paragraph) to any surveillance, inquiries or investigations that are carried out for the purpose of–

(a) obtaining information about a particular person or about the activities or whereabouts of a particular person; or

(b) obtaining information about the circumstances in which or means by which property has been lost or damaged.

(2) This paragraph does not apply to activities carried out exclusively for the purposes of market research.

(3) This paragraph does not apply to activities carried out exclusively for the purpose of determining whether a particular person is credit-worthy.

(4) This paragraph does not apply to any activities of a person with a general qualification within the meaning of section 71 of the Courts and Legal Services Act 1990 (c. 41) which are carried out by him for the purposes of any legal practice carried on–

(a) by him;

(b) by any firm of which he is a partner or by which he is employed;

(c) by any body corporate of which he is a director or member or by which he is employed.

(5) This paragraph does not apply to any activities of a member of a relevant accountancy body which are carried out by him as such and for the purposes of any accountancy practice carried on–

(a) by him;

(b) by any firm of which he is a partner or by which he is employed;

(c) by any body corporate of which he is a director or member or by which he is employed.

(6) This paragraph does not apply to activities carried out for the purpose of obtaining information exclusively with a view to its use, or the use of information to which it relates, for the purposes of or in connection with the publication to the public or to a section of the public of any journalistic, literary or artistic material or of any work of reference.

(7) This paragraph does not apply to activities carried out exclusively by means of references to one or more of the following–

(a) registers or other records that are open (whether or not on the payment of a fee) to public inspection;

(b) registers or other records which are kept by the person by whom or on whose behalf the activities are carried out or to which that person has a right of access;

(c) published works.

(8) This paragraph does not apply to activities carried out with the knowledge or consent of–

(a) the person about whom, or about whose activities or whereabouts, information is sought; or

(b) every person whose interest in any property has been affected by the loss or damage about which information is sought.

(9) This paragraph does not apply to the activities of any person who carries out any inquiries or investigation merely incidentally to the carrying out of any activities which (disregarding this sub-paragraph) are not the activities of a security operative.

(10) In this paragraph 'market research' includes–

(a) discovering whether a person is a potential customer for any goods or services or the extent of his satisfaction with goods or services supplied to him; and

(b) obtaining information from any person for the purpose of analysing public opinion on any matter (whether or not relating to the market for any goods or services).

Security consultants

5(1) This paragraph applies (subject to the following provisions of this paragraph) to the giving of advice about–

(a) the taking of security precautions in relation to any risk to property or to the person; or

(b) the acquisition of any services involving the activities of a security operative.

(2) This paragraph does not apply to the giving of legal or financial advice or to the giving of any advice about the conduct of any business involving the provision of any such services as are mentioned in sub-paragraph (1)(b).

(3) This paragraph does not apply to any activities of a member of a relevant accountancy body which are carried out by him as such and for the purposes of any accountancy practice carried on–

(a) by him;

(b) by any firm of which he is a partner or by which he is employed;

(c) by any body corporate of which he is a director or member or by which he is employed.

(4) This paragraph does not apply to the provision of training to persons for the purpose of giving them qualifications, knowledge or skill for use in the carrying out of the activities of a security operative for others.

Keyholders

6(1) This paragraph applies (subject to the following provisions of this paragraph) to keeping custody of, or controlling access to, any key or similar device for operating (whether mechanically, electronically or otherwise) any lock.

(2) This paragraph does not apply to activities carried out merely incidentally to the provision of any services in connection with a proposal for the sale of any premises or other property to which the key or similar device gives access.

(3) This paragraph does not apply to the activities of a person who holds a key or other device for obtaining access to any premises for purposes incidental to the provision in relation to those premises, or in relation to an individual present on those premises, of any services that do not consist in or include the carrying out of any of the activities of a security operative.

(4) In this paragraph 'lock' means a lock or similar device (whether operated mechanically, electronically or otherwise) that is designed or adapted–

(a) for protecting any premises against unauthorised entry; or

(b) for securing any safe or other container specifically designed or adapted to hold valuables.

PART 2
ACTIVITIES SUBJECT TO ADDITIONAL CONTROLS

General

7(1) Subject to sub-paragraph (2), the activities which are referred to in this Act as activities subject to additional controls are any activities which, so far as they are designated activities, are activities to which any one or more of the following paragraphs of this Part of this Schedule applies.

(2) The Secretary of State may by order amend this Part of this Schedule for the purpose of adding or excluding any such activities as he thinks fit to or from those that fall to be regarded for the purposes of this Act as activities subject to additional controls.

(3) The Secretary of State shall not make an order containing (with or without any other provision) any provision authorised by sub-paragraph (2) unless a draft of the order has been laid before Parliament and approved by a resolution of each House.

Door supervisors etc for public houses, clubs and comparable venues

8(1) This paragraph applies to any activities which are activities of a security operative by virtue of paragraph 2 of this Schedule and are carried out–

(a) in relation to licensed premises; and

(b) at or in relation to times when those premises are open to the public.

(2) In this paragraph 'licensed premises' means (subject to sub-paragraph (3))–

(a) any premises in respect of which a justices' on-licence (within the meaning of the Licensing Act 1964 (c. 26)) is for the time being in force;

(b) any premises comprised in a place to which an occasional licence (within the meaning of that Act) extends;

(c) any premises in respect of which a licence under the Private Places of Entertainment (Licensing) Act 1967 (c. 19) is for the time being in force;

(d) any premises in respect of which a licence under paragraph 1 or 4 of Schedule 1 to the Local Government (Miscellaneous Provisions) Act 1982 (c. 30) or under Schedule 12 to the London Government Act 1963 (c. 33) (licensing of public entertainments) is for the time being in force;

(e) any premises in respect of which a licence of a prescribed description under any prescribed local statutory provision is for the time being in force.

(3) For the purposes of this paragraph premises are not licensed premises in relation to any of the following occasions–

(a) any occasion on which the premises are being used exclusively for the purposes of a club which is registered in respect of those premises under Part 2 of the Licensing Act 1964, other than an occasion on which a certificate under section 79 of that Act (music and dancing) is for the time being in force in respect of those premises;

(b) any occasion on which a Part 4 licence (within the meaning of that Act of 1964) is in force in respect of the premises (restaurants and guest houses) and they are being used wholly or mainly for the purposes by reference to which they are premises for which such a licence may be granted;

(c) any occasion on which a licence is in force in respect of the premises under the Theatres Act 1968 (c. 54);

(d) any occasion on which letters patent of the Crown make it lawful for those premises to be used for the public performance of plays without a licence under that Act of 1968;

(e) any occasion on which a licence is in force in respect of the premises under the Gaming Act 1968 (c. 65) and the premises are being used wholly or mainly for the purposes of gaming to which Part 2 of that Act applies;

(f) any occasion on which a licence is in force in respect of the premises under the Cinemas Act 1985 (c. 13) and they are being used wholly or mainly for the purposes for which such a licence is required; or

(g) any such other occasion as may be prescribed for the purposes of this sub-paragraph.

(4) For the purposes of this paragraph the times when premises are open to the public shall be taken to include any time when they are open to a section of the public comprising the individuals who qualify for admission to the premises as the members of a particular club, association or group or otherwise as being persons to whom a particular description applies or in relation to whom particular conditions are satisfied.

(5) References in this paragraph to the occasion on which any premises are being used for a particular purpose include references to any time on that occasion when the premises are about to be used for that purpose, or have just been used for that purpose.

Immobilisation of vehicles

9   This paragraph applies to any activities which are activities of a security operative by virtue of paragraph 3 of this Schedule.

APPENDIX 7

MEMBERS OF THE SECURITY INDUSTRY AUTHORITY

Molly Meacher. Formerly Deputy Chairperson of the Police Complaints Authority. Appointed as Chairman of the Security Industry Authority (SIA) on 1 April 2002.

The following had their appointments to the board of the SIA announced on 2 April 2003:

Richard Childs. Chief Constable of the Lincolnshire Police. Appointed for three years, part-time, as the representative of the Association of Chief Police Officers.

Robin Dahlberg. Appointed for four years, part-time. Has 30 years' international experience as a business systems director.

Peter Hermitage. Appointed for four years, part-time. Former director of National Police Training. Currently Chairman of East Kent NHS Hospitals Trust and Governor of Christchurch University College, Canterbury.

Brendan O'Friel. Appointed for four years, part-time. Former prison governor. Currently Chairman of the North Western Rail Passengers Committee, a member of employment tribunals and a member of Cheshire Area Probation Board.

Bruce Warman. Appointed for four years, part-time. Currently a member of the Employment Appeal Tribunal. Chairs committees in the Confederation of British Industry on employment policy issues. Was recently the personnel director for Vauxhall Motors.

The Chief Executive of the SIA is **John Saunders**, who was appointed on 1 April 2002. His background includes experience with the business link, training and enterprise council.

INDEX